As the Father Has Sent Me

As the Father Has Sent Me

God's Progress of Redemption: Part One

Rod Culbertson

FOREWORD BY
Jim Hatch

WIPF & STOCK · Eugene, Oregon

AS THE FATHER HAS SENT ME
God's Progress of Redemption

Wipf & Stock
An Imprint of Wipf and Stock Publishers
199 W. 8th Ave., Suite 3
Eugene, OR 97401

www.wipfandstock.com

PAPERBACK ISBN: 978-1-5326-4903-5
HARDCOVER ISBN: 978-1-5326-4904-2
EBOOK ISBN: 978-1-5326-4905-9

Manufactured in the U.S.A.

Dedication

WITH LIFELONG GRATITUDE AND indebtedness, and having been blessed beyond measure to be taught by and know the man (and his wife, Mittie), I dedicate this book to the greatest professor that I have ever heard teach— Mr. James "Buck" Hatch.

"Buck" Hatch was a man broken by life, humble, self-deprecating, and constitutionally insecure. Yet he was a holy and useful vessel in the hands of God, who had graciously redeemed him. His brokenness enhanced his ministry of teaching, preaching, and counseling. His security was found in Christ! At times, he seemed nervous to teach, as well as embarrassed at the thought that, in his unworthiness, he would have anything worthwhile to tell his students. Yet, God's strength was perfected in "Buck" Hatch's weakness, and we listened as if the next moment of life depended upon every word he spoke. The man was intense about Christ! He taught me about the prophets (whom he loved), family life and marriage, and through his legendary course, "Progress of Redemption," he shaped my life and ministry forever. "Buck" Hatch also became my personal counselor during the throes of challenging pastoral ministry, pastoral work that was often attended with much personal introspection and questioning.

Truly, I can still hear him declaring the poignant chapel message he delivered at Columbia International University (then Columbia Bible College) from 1 Corinthians 3:9 during my senior year of seminary. He reiterated to those of us preparing to serve God in full-time ministry, "You are God's cultivated field!" I knew that "Buck" Hatch believed it, and ever since I have believed it—I am God's work! And so is his church. I must humbly add that this book is mostly "Buck" Hatch's work, written with hopes that his ministry will continue to bear fruit in God's kingdom and be a blessing to his church.

Contents

Illustrations

Foreword

MELLOW AND GRATEFUL. READING my friend Rod Culbertson's *As the Father Has Sent Me* left me with both feelings.

On the one hand, of course my dad's teaching permeates this book. So as I write this, I'm mellow—I miss him! And I share Rod's view of him as a teacher. He was indeed the best teacher I've ever learned under. That flowed from his absolute aversion to teaching as a "monological information dump" and his determination that students themselves have the "Aha!" experience. Staying riveted to that objective radically impacted his teaching. This was perhaps uniquely true in what for many became their favorite course under Buck Hatch, Progress of Redemption. So I kept seeing and hearing dad as I read this book.

But the other sense is equally true. I'm deeply grateful for Rod's effective and biblical unpacking of this foundational teaching of Buck Hatch. To be sure, Rod's personal context, analysis, and life illustrations make this work his very own in a winsome way. To see clearly again the biblical flow of the purposes of God in the Scriptures, particularly in the Old Testament, will be very helpful to any who read. Far too many see the Bible as atomistic individual "pieces," and rarely ever grasp what the Lord is doing from the beginning to the end of Scripture. Dad's (and Rod's!) reminder of the ways the Lord works—he has a plan, takes his time, uses fallible human instruments to change the world—are energizing.

I'm grateful that this broader understanding can be expanded through *As the Father Has Sent Me.* I warmly commend it to you.

Jim Hatch

Preface

GOD ALWAYS HAS A plan and his plan will play out in a well-orchestrated story for the world. As a matter of fact, this world is his world and the world's story is a story that God is both "writing" and working out by his sovereign and powerful hand, through the power of the Holy Spirit. This book, *As The Father Has Sent Me*, is the first of two books that will summarize God's plan of redemption (saving a people for himself to the honor of his own glory and majesty). Both books will demonstrate to the reader how God's story unfolds according to his gracious plan. *As The Father Has Sent Me* will start in the beginning, commonly known as the book of Genesis, and will climax in its narrative with the coming of Christ, the Son of God. You will watch God's "drama of redemption" unfold before your eyes as you read the text of book one. The second book, *So Send I You*, will continue the story with Christ's command to his disciples to make other disciples (or followers) of the entire world. As you read *So Send I You*, you will watch the beginning of God's movement from saving the nation of Israel for his own purposes to the calling of a special people to himself from the ranges of the entire world. So, I must prepare the reader for the inevitable: when you complete this volume, you will not be finished with the entire story. Book one, *As The Father Has Sent Me*, is filled with all sorts of insights about both the Bible and God's plan, but at its completion, although you will crescendo to the apex of the message, the coming of Christ, the story will not be over. Hopefully, you will want to continue reading and will pursue the second book, *So Send I You*. And if you engage in reading volume two, you could even discover that you—yes, you yourself—might make an appearance in God's story as well. So, I hope you will enjoy both books and in doing so, find yourself in the midst of God's story for the world.

Acknowledgments

I ONCE MET WITH an old friend, and minister at the time, whom I knew while we were both students at the University of South Carolina. When he mentioned to me that he had earned his Master of Divinity (and ThM) degree at Dallas Theological Seminary, I remarked, "Oh, you were able to study under the great Christian education professor, Dr. Howard Hendricks. That must have been incredible!" His reply was simply this, "Yes, but I envy your studies at Columbia International University. You were able to study under the legendary 'Buck' Hatch! There is no one like him!" And he was correct—I had learned from a master teacher.

In my dedication, I have acknowledged that the bulk of this work is a product of the instruction of Presbyterian minister, Reverend Mr. James "Buck" Hatch, Professor of Bible, among other things, at Columbia International University. This book primarily consists of notes from his insightful course, "Progress of Redemption," a course well known to a vast number of the graduates of CIU. I have tried to recapture the course and enhance it with some of my own insights. Ultimately, the material is a reproduction of his teaching, straight from the copious notes I took covering the first portion of his "Progress of Redemption" course. Therefore, credit goes to Mr. Hatch, the man who kept us both attentive and alert by constantly stopping his lectures with long pauses, while matter-of-factly saying, "Look up here!" And we did!

Many thanks are due to my professional graphics artist for creating some very nice pictures that enhance this work. Kirby McCreight is a very gifted graphics man who provided both T-shirt graphics and logos while involved in my RUF ministry at the University of Florida in the 1980's. He was gracious enough to provide his generous assistance and expertise for this book. I am very grateful to Christ for Kirby and his willingness to serve in this project.

I also must thank my teaching assistant at Reformed Theological Seminary, Ms. Anna Unkefer, who provided the gift of perfection and tenacity necessary to publish a book such as this one. I am deeply grateful for her work on my behalf. Finally, I appreciate those readers who assisted me in editing the work and bringing clarity to my thoughts on paper: Mrs. Wendy Howell Thomas and Mrs. Tari Williamson.

Introduction

As a young boy I grew up next door to a celebrity of sorts. My uncle, John Bolt Culbertson, was a well-known lawyer and aspiring politician who often made the news due to his flamboyant, verbose, and colorful personality, along with a platform that revolved around the need to take care of the poor, disenfranchised, and defenseless citizens of South Carolina. It has been said that, in my home state, he made both Democrats and Republicans furious. He was a famous individual in his era (particularly the 1960s and 1970s) and also carried a reputation as a life-loving man who could throw a big party for his legal and political friends, eating and enjoying their company in first-class fashion (I know; I attended some of those parties!)

But what I might remember most was that he lived in an extremely unique rock mansion, much of which I watched (and played in) while it was being built. As a seven or eight-year-old, I recall that various materials were deposited constantly in my uncle's long, narrow front yard. In a matter of a few months, there were stacks of wooden I-beams, piles of rocks, and mounds of dirt sitting next door in his front yard (I still have photos). As kids, my brother and I, and our friends would have fun around these piles, sometimes playing "king of the hill" on the dirt mounds. We knew that Uncle John was going to use these materials to add to his already unusual mansion but to us, these lumps of material were mostly an eyesore and an occasional playground. We wondered, "What will become of all of this junk?"

As children, what we did not have, at least not explicitly, was the vision for what these piles of debris could become. My Uncle John knew what he wanted and could see the big picture of a huge house, much larger than what he already had. Eventually (and it took many years), the piles of dirt, stone, and lumber would become an incredible addition to his already remarkable mansion. Uncle John added a large bathroom containing a sunken bathtub, a huge kitchen suitable for cooking large meals for the groups he and his wife frequently hosted, and a bedroom with an elevated area for the bed. Upstairs he created a guest room for the friends of his younger children (supplied with around ten single beds—all decorated the same: with red, white, and blue bedspreads), and a chapel containing a small pulpit and wooden pews for sitting. Then there was the spellbinding two-tiered white and powder puff blue lady's wardrobe room filled with doors on every wall on both tiers. The wardrobe room contained mirrors on every door, as well as a spiral staircase to reach the closets on the second tier of the room. Those were the most distinguished additions, but there was also a large screened-in porch, a huge two car carport, a laundry room, and an area that could function as a greenhouse. Little did we realize what would be created out of those piles of rubble and wood; in time, a huge mansion would be built!

And so it is with God's kingdom. God is at work in his world and he has a plan, as well as a blueprint for the undertaking of that plan. His plan is huge, thoughtful, and precise! But often, when we read about his plan in the Bible, we are confused and uncertain about what he is actually doing. We read the books in the Bible, attempt to piece together the different names and events, and often do so without clarity of understanding or having any concept of the chronology of biblical times or its people. Just like my friends and I gazing at my uncle's messy front yard, we look at all of the oblique parts of the Bible and have no sense of the big picture or the grand storyline that is ultimately going to unfold. How can we put together this complicated puzzle?

Why This Book?

The purpose of this book is to help the reader to both understand and discover the wonderful plan of God as it unfolds through the narrative of Scripture. This book is both a look at the history of God's plan of redemption and a work that attempts to clarify how God has worked out his redemptive plan here on earth. Anything that God does is amazing! And I believe you will be amazed to read about and observe the plan of God as he calls a people to himself. Many people understand that the cross of Christ is central to the plan of God. But the cross did not come out of nowhere. The effects of the cross are intended to shake the earth! And we will watch that happen just as God intended it to.

You may be pleased to hear that this book will not contain explicit and intricate explanations of theology. There will be an occasional doctrinal explanation, but the text will not dwell on concepts like "the ramifications of supralapsarianism" or "the dispensational scheme of eschatology!" Whew—I know you are now breathing a deep sigh of relief! Read on and you will see that ultimately this book will encompass the Bible's history. We will cover the entire Old Testament and take a glimpse into the New, but primarily, we will be using *concepts* to do so. There are 1189 chapters in the Bible. Those chapter divisions (which are a product of a man made system for organizing biblical information) are broken up into 31,173 verses. Depending upon one's translation, the Bible contains over 770,000 words, as well as over three and one-half million letters. From the individual letters of the text (written in Greek, Hebrew, and a little Aramaic) to each of the individual sixty-six books, the Bible is the book of books, having been inspired in the whole by the Holy Spirit. Yet, we will not focus on every letter, word, paragraph, or chapter, but only on the concepts that help us understand how God's redemptive plan is unfolding, so do not be overwhelmed by the massive composition that is known as the Bible.

I once read about a minister who spent his total preaching career with only one church while preaching through the entire Bible verse-by-verse and chapter-by-chapter. His ministry preaching through the entire Bible lasted fifty-two years! We're not going to do that! And I want to be clear—this is not a verse-by-verse or chapter-by-chapter study. Furthermore, this book is not a study of various topics or subjects, such as looking at what the Scriptures say about "faith," "salvation," "love," or "grace." As fun as that might be, we will not take the time to peruse the various texts that speak to a given topic. Nor will this be an overview of each and every book of the Bible, although we will overview a few; many other well written books provide that service. Even though one goal of every Christian should be to understand the purpose or key point of *each* of the sixty-six books of the Bible, we will not fulfill that laudable goal in this endeavor.

The goal of this book is to provide a survey of God's grand plan of redemption. This survey will not be comprehensive, nor will it answer every question. As we watch the story of the Bible unfold, we will learn more through concepts than through detailed explanations. We will study the relationships between the materials but will not look closely at those relationships through microanalysis (scholars call that detailed study "exegesis"). We will see the big picture storyline but will not dwell upon the many individual stories unless they are crucial to conveying the concepts involved. The focus of this book will be upon the *unity* of the Bible, a unity that is based upon the *actions* of God. The Bible is a history book, tracing God's actions upon the earth. That history culminates in the revelation of God's Son, Jesus Christ. Someone once said, "History is His Story!" I would agree and together we will see his story unfold, guided by the hand of a sovereign and benevolent God, whom his people can affectionately call "Father."

Lessons to Be Learned

As we become engaged in God's story, we will learn some poignant lessons about God. Some of those lessons will include the following:

1. God takes his time—he patiently works to build something good. We need to be patient with God's plan because he is patient in developing it. (We often have to apply this lesson to our own lives and personal circumstances as well.)

2. God works with individuals, but in doing so, he affects the world! One person can make a difference in God's world if God's grace is involved in the life of that person.

3. God is sovereign over history. He is involved in the little things (including our lives) and the large things (the nations). He is sovereign over time, matter, places, and persons. The Christian and biblical worldview is not deism. Deism suggests that God created the world, then wound it up like a watch, letting it tick away. In deism, God has removed his involvement in the world and its activities. We will discover that God is *very* involved in both our lives and the world.

4. God uses the sin (disobedience) of man (men and women, corporately and individually) to do his will. This lesson brings us much consolation, since sin is so often the bi-product of our own lives. God can overcome our sins, failures, rebellions, and their consequences if he so chooses. That thought brings us to our next lesson.

5. God is gracious despite our sin. He can bring (or produce) something good even out of his own people's sin. We will see that God does that often. He is a God of grace!

6. God's people do some horrible things. Some of the actions of God's people are inexcusable and often they know better. But God disciplines his people, though he is frequently very gracious in the process. Sometimes his discipline is unimaginable to us, but fully understandable when we begin to grasp what a truly holy and perfect God he is.

7. Nothing seems to come easy for those who are a part of God's kingdom. God's plan is not always clearly revealed, nor are his ways easy to fathom or follow.

8. God is goal oriented. God has a certain goal that he will reach and he has a plan to make it happen. We will look at that goal in a moment.

9. God's plan will bring optimism to our lives as Christians. If God's plan is good and he is ultimately going to glorify himself and fill the earth with his glory, then we can look forward with positive anticipation to what he is going to do.

10. We will be encouraged by the overall benefit of this study. We will see God's plan in a much clearer light. We will understand our Bibles in a much greater way. And hopefully, we will have a firmer grasp of our place in God's redemptive plan and will thus act upon it. We will be amazed by God's plan for the world and for our lives!

I'm sure that there will be many other lessons to be learned from this study but I am confident that we will benefit from those listed above!

The Goal

As we move forward in our study of God's redemptive plan, we will be guided by the continual thought and question of *progress*. We will look for and evaluate the progress of God's plan in history. We will watch God as he moves forward and we will wait to see if the unfolding plan of God brings progress to his goal for all of the earth. We will discover that God's ways are radically different from our ways (Isa 55:8). We will be able to find God's stated goal for the earth in a number of passages, all contained within the Old Testament. His goal is not only mentioned more than once, but it also is expressed in a variety of literary types. We will see the stated goal pop up at least four times in the Old Testament. God's plan for mankind and the world in which he lives is worded simply in Habakkuk 2:14, "For the earth will be filled with the knowledge of the glory of the LORD as the waters cover the sea." Filling the earth with the glory of the Lord is quite the goal. Yet, this is what God has been doing from the beginning of time. We will observe his plan throughout this book. A goal is normally not reached right after it is immediately set, especially a goal this large. But in order for a huge goal to become accomplished, one must begin somewhere. And so God starts with a seed. Given time and the proper circumstances for growth, a seed will eventually become something very large. An acorn can become an oak tree. A fertilized egg can become a grown, fully functioning human being. God's planted seed can grow into world-wide glory. A seed has vast potential for the future. A seed is simple but leads into the complex. There is the potential in a seed for everything which is involved in the final product.

The Seed

Some years ago, I had to make a very difficult, even painful, decision. I had to cut down an oak tree that had grown over the years just a few yards from the side of my house. Unfortunately, this oak tree, which was probably seven or eight decades old, had become hollow inside, its hollowness starting a few feet at the bottom and running up the middle of the trunk, creating a possible hazard for the safety of our house. We had already lost an older, larger oak tree due to an immense wind storm a few years earlier and I felt threatened. So, despite the beauty of the oak, the shade it provided, and the respect and love I have for trees, I paid handsomely to have it taken down. The next spring, however, something unexpected happened. A few weeks after spring arrived, around a hundred or so oak seedlings sprouted out of the ground where the shadows of that huge oak previously had stood. Maybe that is nature's way; I don't know. I told a group of our RTS students about what had happened with the seedlings and as a result, one of our administrators heard about it. She came up to me afterward and said, "I would like some of those seedlings to plant in my yard." I told her I would bring some to the school soon. I went out and dug up about a two square foot piece of soil and placed it in a large cardboard box. Contained within it were around 8–10 six-inch-high oak seedlings. When I delivered it to her the next day, I amusingly stated, "Here are your oak trees!" Of course, they were only seedlings, but each sprig had the potential of becoming, in time, a huge oak tree. She was thrilled to have them. They were only seedlings, which had begun as mere seeds or acorns, but each of them contained "oak tree" potential. We shall see that God's seed in his redemptive plan is much like those acorns, containing vast potential for growth beyond comprehension.

Similarly, in the 1970s, in Gainesville, Florida, a young male college student attending the University of Florida appeared at the Sunday morning worship service in a small Presbyterian church plant that was meeting in a private school on the west side of town. The young man's name was Joe. The college-town church he attended that day was meager in size, consisting of less than fifty people. When Joe showed up, he was readily noticed as a college student. After that morning, someone in the church excitedly stated, "We have a college student—let's start a college ministry!" Obviously, it is very difficult to begin a college ministry with only one student, but that is what Faith Presbyterian Church did that day when Joe from Pensacola showed up. Joe was the "seed" of what that college ministry would become. Eventually, a handful of other Florida students joined both Joe and Faith Church. In time, others attended and the group grew to around twenty. They called the college ministry "Faith Fellowship." In time, the church decided to call a full-time assistant pastor to serve these college students. As he and his wife worked in this challenging campus environment, the group continued to grow. And although the ministry (eventually known as Reformed University Fellowship or RUF) never became numerically large, over the years it would expand around the state of Florida to its present day status of seven campus ministries on seven significant Florida college campuses. Who could have imagined seven vibrant campus ministries all over the state of Florida in those early days at Faith Presbyterian Church when just one college student showed up to the church service? As the first college student bedding down at Faith church, Joe was the seed of a work that has constantly and steadily grown, and one that, Lord willing, will continue to grow and expand in the future.

In God's plan, the seed is a promise. We will hear the promise stated later as it is delivered in timely fashion. The goal is that the earth will be filled with the knowledge of the glory of God. The goal is both massive and magnificent. Buck Hatch says that the goal is fulfilled through God working in his people, a people who both love God and one another. Can you imagine millions, even billions, of people truly loving the God of the universe? Can you imagine those same people loving their brothers and sisters in Christ, loving their neighbors as themselves, and loving even their enemies? Only God, through his Holy Spirit, can make this happen on a world-wide scale.

The light of God will shine in the darkness, but it will take time. Progress in God's plan is sure to occur, though sometimes in the most unlikely scenarios. The goal is still being reached and we are part of it!

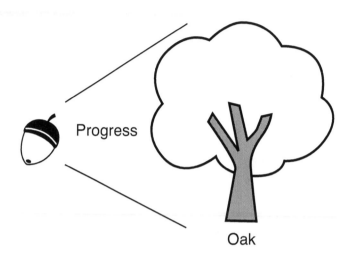

Progress

Oak

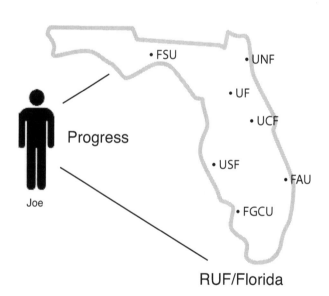

Progress

Joe

RUF/Florida

The Unity of Scripture

The simplest definition of unity is "the state of being one." Unity means oneness. A piece of chalk is one. Any part of it can be used to draw on a chalk
board (remember those?) or on driveway pavement. Chalk is chalk! It has
organic (or essential) unity in its nature as chalk. But consider an ink pen.
There is unity in an ink pen, but that unity is due to the functional aspects
of the ink pen. It has functional unity. The ink pen needs ink, a chamber to
hold the ink, a ball bearing (or ballpoint tip) that rolls the ink out on paper,
and a plastic barrel encasing the chamber, normally accompanied by a cap
for the pen (and possibly a pen grip). The pen has unity only in its functional
parts. It normally could not be used unless it has all the essential parts in
working order. United properly together, the parts become an ink pen that
functions correctly. This unity demonstrates the unity of the Bible.

The Scriptures are very diverse and yet they function with one purpose—to proclaim the living God's plan to glorify himself. The diversity of
Scripture is seen in the types of literature found in these books—books of
history, law, poetry, prophecy, and gospel. There are genres (or categories)
of Scripture: parables, symbolism, narrative, wisdom, and apocalyptic (end
times) literature. There are extensive writings of theology and doctrine, as
well as letters (or epistles) written to both individuals and groups of people.
The Bible is comprised of sixty-six books. The books were written by forty
different authors over a period of fifteen hundred years, in three different
languages (mostly Hebrew and Greek) and thirteen different countries. To
take a major piece of literature as diverse as the Bible and make it functional
requires the touch (or authorship) of God, who is himself the "three in one"!
The oneness of diversity is seen in our own humanity. As people, we are
both body and soul, yet we function as one being. In marriage, we find male
united to female; they are different, i.e., diverse, yet become one in flesh. In
the church, the Apostle Paul reminds the churches at Ephesus (chapter 4)
and Corinth (chapter 12) that although they have various members with
diverse gifts, they are united as one in Christ. How amazing is unity in diversity? Buck Hatch says, "All the books of the Bible come together without
collusion (planning between parties) or collision (contradiction)."

The unity of Scripture is based on this one key principle: God initiates
his plan. God is at work in his world; he is not passive. God deals with men
and women here on the earth! When we speak of the unity of Scripture, we
are dealing with history because biblical history demonstrates that God is
present and working. When I was a campus minister at the University of

Florida, each year during both the summer and winter campus breaks, I received training from my campus ministry, Reformed University Fellowship, and its founder, Reverend Mr. Mark Lowrey. As a fledgling campus ministry for our denomination, we all had much to learn. Thankfully, in Mark Lowrey, we had a campus ministry genius training us. He taught so many concepts and so much philosophy of ministry that we could not keep up with him. But he was very helpful to all who would listen. And there was one concept that he reiterated time and time again at every staff training session. You could not miss it. He constantly reminded us of this one reality, a truth that we sometimes forgot or simply did not believe as we labored. Mark would always remind us of this: "God is at work!" "God is at work" is what we heard year after year, especially as we wondered if he really was at work, particularly among us campus ministers who were travailing in difficult soil. This is the idea that brings unity to Scripture—God is acting; God is working. He is the author of history and is actively taking initiative upon the earth. Buck Hatch submits that although the Bible is divided into the Old Testament and the New Testament, we should actually think of the Scriptures as being divided into two *historical* eras. God raises up his church among the people of Israel and then adds the Gentiles to the story. Simply stated, the Bible is an unfolding drama, a story that can be followed. The historical material of the Bible, by definition, is "that infallible record of what God initiates to do with mankind on earth." History is a record of God's acting and working among us! God's historical record is observed as a linear timeline that has a beginning, proceeds forward, and will one day be completed. History is "the great operation of God!"

Speaking and Acting

When we read the Scriptures, we discover that God communicates to his people in two possible ways. As noted above, he acts in this world. He makes history. But, we also find large portions of Scripture (sometimes whole books) in which God delivers extensive messages—quite simply, he speaks. The book of Nehemiah is historical in nature. Psalms are written discourse. The books of Isaiah and Matthew include both speaking and acting (or doing). God speaks and he acts. We see this combination in various texts:

- Numbers 23:19, "God is not man, that he should lie, or a son of man, that he should change his mind. Has he *said*, and will he not *do* it? Or has he *spoken*, and will he not *fulfill* it?"

- Amos 3:7, "For the Lord God *does* nothing without *revealing* his secret to his servants the prophets."

- Matthew 11:2–4, "Now when John heard in prison about the deeds of the Christ, he sent word by his disciples and said to him, 'Are you the one who is to come, or shall we look for another?' And Jesus answered them, 'Go and tell John what you *hear* and *see.*'"

- Acts 1:1, "In the first book, O Theophilus, I have dealt with all that Jesus began to *do* and *teach* . . ." (Italics mine, for emphasis)

When we consider the "God who speaks," we think of concepts such as prophecy, gospel, discourse, the Sermon on the Mount, messages in the book of Acts by Peter, Stephen, and Paul, etc. We also think about the word "revelation." God reveals himself by condescending and speaking to us through his chosen messengers. The speaking sections of the Bible may be greater in proportion than the historical sections, but when we read the historical sections, we realize that *the unity of the Bible consists in God acting!* The actions of God are very significant. We read about how God intervenes on behalf of his people, particularly in his saving acts. We see God's miracles and view them with awe. We see him sending his Son as the savior of the world and can hardly believe it. Buck Hatch says that Jesus's death is more important than anything Christ says. Surely, sending his Son into the world, sacrificing him on the cross, and raising him from the dead is the greatest *act* that God the Father has ever done! History is not a record of what God says; it is a record of what God does. In what does the unity of the Bible consist? That unity is derived from God's historical revelation, which is culminated in the coming of Christ.

Progress

As we walk through God's unfolding plan of redemption, we will find ourselves asking the essential question, "Is *this* progress?" That is, we hope to discover whether we are moving forward and advancing toward the grand goal that God has set forth. Progress in our context will describe the fact that God is moving forward, that he is making positive things happen in regard to his plan and in his world. We will also wonder about how he is moving forward. The reality is that God does not operate or think as we do—his definition of progress might very well differ from ours. As Isaiah writes, "For my thoughts are not your thoughts, neither are your ways my ways, declares the LORD" (Isa 55:8). His thinking and his ways (acts) are radically different from ours. The basic premises of the "progress theme" are: 1) God is, 2) God is alive, 3) God gives life to things, and finally, 4) these things grow. The progress we observe will move from a small beginning to a final goal. The progress will be measured by steps, moving (almost without exception) in a forward direction. At some point in time, progress, just as an infant becomes a child and then an adult, will cease or stop. If we do not understand the goal, we will not be able to understand the steps of progress. Throughout this study, we must constantly keep the goal in mind and evaluate the progress by the movement toward the goal: "That God will fill the earth with the knowledge of his glory" (Hab 2:14). God's goal will take place on the earth, as God shows us how wonderful he is through his church, the people he gathers together here on the earth. How will this happen? God will demonstrate his glory by calling a people together who will love God with all of their hearts and in turn, will love one another as themselves.

In The Beginning

"In the beginning, God created the heavens and the earth" (Gen 1:1). These are the first words of the Bible and are so famous and notable that they were quoted on Christmas Eve in 1968 in outer space! Three American astronauts, James Lovell, Frank Borman, and Bill Anders, the first astronauts to ever circle the moon in a spacecraft, took turns reciting the first ten verses of Genesis chapter 1 during the Apollo 8 space flight. One billion people, the largest television audience in the world at that time, watched and listened as they read. Genesis 1:1 is an acclaimed verse, no matter what the reader believes about it. Similarly, chapters 1–11 of Genesis are not only significant in their poignancy but are foundational to everything else that the Bible tells us, especially as we seek to understand the progress of God's plan of redemption on earth. These eleven chapters tell us everything we need to know about the reason for God's plan. They do not explain everything we want to know about a multitude of questions that arise when we look at the origins of both created things and humankind, but what they do tell us is very compelling. Explaining every question about life is not the purpose of the first eleven chapters of the Bible. Explaining our greatest need, however, is that purpose.

If we take a cursory read of Genesis chapters 1–11, we could break it down into three sections with eleven different emphases. Those would be:

Section One

- Chapter 1: Creation of the universe/world and man; everything is good, even very good!
- Chapter 2: A detailed account of the creation of man and woman

- Chapter 3: The disobedience of man (mankind) through the first temptation and sin

- Chapter 4: The first murder—the sin nature of man is passed along to his posterity

- Chapter 5: A *genealogy* is written, tracing the ancestry from Adam to Noah

Section Two

- Chapter 6: The utter wickedness of all mankind everywhere and the call for Noah's ark

- Chapter 7: The entire world, except for Noah and his family, who are saved, as well as pairs of animals, is destroyed by a world-wide flood

- Chapter 8: The flood ceases and Noah leaves the ark

- Chapter 9: Noah is commanded to replenish the earth and is given the sign of the covenant in the form of a rainbow that God will never flood the entire world again

- Chapter 10: A *genealogy* is written, tracing the ancestry of Noah through his three sons Shem, Ham, and Japheth

Section Three

- Chapter 11 (part one): The building of the tower of Babel, the confusion of languages, as well as the scattering of peoples over the face of the whole earth

- Chapter 11 (part two): A *genealogy* of Shem to Terah, father of Abram, is provided, introducing Abram and his wife Sarai, who is barren

These three sections, which are divided by selective genealogies tying them together, might be summarized by the following three words:

- Chapters 1–4: Disobedience

- Chapters 6–9: Destruction

- Chapter 11 (part one): Dispersion

The world was initially a good place created by a great God. It was inhabited by two people who were especially created for this world. These two people, one man and one woman, were designed for procreation. They were created possessing original righteousness, holiness, and a disposition

14

to know, love, and walk with God. And their hearts were made to obey their creator. At the end of Genesis chapter 1, we are told that all of God's creation, including the pinnacle of creation, man and woman, is very good! The phrase "very good" is extremely important to the text because it describes God's original creation and the context in which the man and woman can thrive. However, once we quickly move to the third chapter of Genesis, the text presents us with the problem that ruins man's perfect world consisting of a constant, loving relationship to God. The man and his wife sin against God by partaking of the forbidden fruit. Chapter 3 of Genesis is not only one of the most crucial narratives in the Bible, it is actually one of the most believable, as we observe our world throughout history, including up to the present day. Sin, moral failure, injustice, selfishness, and godlessness prevail around the world. Simply stated, theologians call this failure to obey God, "the Fall." The sin of the first man and first woman (the first married couple) led to sibling rivalry and the first murder in God's world. Chapter 4 may cause many questions to surface in the reader's mind, but one thing is clear: the Fall had consequences. The sin nature was passed on. The storyline has gone from "very good" to "disobedience brings tragic consequences." We might characterize chapters 3 and 4 as "not good, not very good at all!"

Following the first genealogy of Genesis, we come to the account of the flood and Noah's deliverance. This description of what Adam and Eve's sin has, in time, eventually authored must be noted: "The LORD saw that the *wickedness* of man was *great* in the earth, and that *every* intention of the thoughts of his heart was *only evil continually*" (Gen 6:5; italics mine, for emphasis). Pervasive wickedness now exists on a massive, comprehensive scale. Evil consumes the minds and intentions of all mankind and the earth is filled with violence. This is the continuous state of life on God's once very good earth. In four quick chapters, we are given an account regarding humanity which consists of a horrific nature. The corruption is so vast that God resolves to start over. In judgment, he will not spare anyone except Noah and his family, the tokens of his grace and favor. Chapters 6–9 are filled with a dark cloud of sin and destruction, brightened only by a silver lining that is the grace of God.

Following the second genealogy of Genesis, we read the third section of the first eleven chapters, a brief account of the building of the tower of Babel. The essence of this story is that mankind has not learned what it means to seek their creator and to fill the earth with the knowledge of his glory. Rather, we read a story about a strategy to build a single city with a huge tower representing not only the self-exaltation of humanity, but also a spirit of resisting God's will. From the first "battle of wills" in the garden, mankind has sought to make a name for himself. This self-seeking spirit, along with the failure to spread out and fill the entire earth with people who can know and honor God, is opposed by God, who uses the confusion of languages to prevent their endeavor. The origin of diverse languages is not the primary point of the narrative. The continuation of both rebelliousness against God, as well as failure to spread his image throughout the world is the focus of the story. If they will not scatter and fill the earth, God will scatter them and use language to do so.

So, now we must ask ourselves the ever pervasive question of the book. Looking at Genesis chapters 1–11, we surmise, "Do we see progress?" Is God moving forward in his redemptive plan? Is God's glory spreading over all the earth thus far? As we give the question some thought, we think of how he covered Adam and Eve with an animal skin in place of the garments of their own making, the loincloth made of fig leaves. But is this progress? We might postulate that God's saving of Noah and his family from the flood through the provision of the ark could be progress of some sort. We might think that the promise of a deliverer in Genesis 3:15 or the covenant rainbow and its promise of God's restraint of cataclysmic judgment is progress as well. But if we are honest in following the development of the events in the first eleven chapters of Genesis, we must come to the conclusion that what started out as "very good," and with vast potential, has quickly turned, in the narrative, into terribly bad. There is no progress to be seen. So, what is the purpose of these eleven chapters?

These beginning chapters of Genesis are not trying to answer every question of origin, although they do answer many questions. Their primary purpose is to set the stage for what God needs, and is going, to do in the world in the future. These chapters of the Bible are unique. Moses explains that the world *needs* help. These chapters show us the *need* in a fallen world. These chapters set the stage for the redemptive plan. God is moving toward the goal, but mankind is not—when our original parents sinned, they passed on their sin nature with devastating effect (sibling rivalry, ending in murder). Eventually, *all* people practice wickedness and evil continually, so much so that they are destroyed by God in the flood. And even after an event of such seismic proportion, mankind pursues its own exaltation at Babel, elevating itself and opposing the will of God to fill the earth with his glory.

Clearly we do not observe progress in these chapters. We see sin and disobedience, along with a universal curse; we see wickedness and destruction; and we see the rebellious dispersed in confusion. These chapters are the *prologue* for the remainder of the biblical story. These chapters demonstrate *the great need* on earth. They explain what has happened prior to the intervention that God will initiate in Genesis chapter 12. They prepare the listener (the original audience was the people of Israel, having been liberated from Egypt) for the action that will follow. These chapters present the dark, dismal setting of life on earth and prepare the listener for the raising of the curtain. These chapters comprise the prologue.

A prologue is an introduction, a preface, or a forward to a literary, theatrical, or musical work. A prologue often creates anticipation, and even suspense or intrigue. When I was a young boy, my favorite television program (and still my favorite of all time) was a 1960s series known as "The Fugitive," starring David Janssen as Dr. Richard Kimble. Dr. Kimble was always on the run, having been falsely accused of murdering his wife (the show was based on the real life events of one Dr. Samuel Sheppard). The weekly plots were always engaging due to the melancholic acting of David Janssen and the drama of constant chase by the law. One of the best parts of the program for me, however, was always the opening scene. For twenty seconds to a minute, a scene of action was portrayed that often included intense drama and a trial of some sort. Trouble was surely in store for the much sought after Dr. Kimble. What would happen next? Would his nemesis, Lt. Philip Gerard, finally capture him? Would he get a glimpse of the real killer, the ever elusive one-armed man? Watch this episode and find out! This opening scene was the prologue to the rest of the night's program, skillfully capturing the audience's attention. Genesis chapters 1–11 are the beginning of the redemptive story, but serve as the prologue. These first few stories simply set the stage for what is to come. This opening biblical scene, moving from grandeur to seeming hopelessness, is told as the very frank prologue introducing the remainder of a marvelous story. Under the circumstances, the listener or reader wonders, "will the goal be reached?" "Is anything good going to happen with all of this trouble on earth?" Act one, scene one is soon to commence!

1-4	5	6-9	10	11	11
FALL Disobedience	Genealogy	**FLOOD** Destruction	Genealogy	**BABEL** Dispersion	Genealogy

GENESIS 1-11
PROLOGUE: SIN
MAN'S NEED FOR REDEMPTION

Act One, Scene One

As we observed in the previous chapter, the beginning chapters of the Bible are radically different from the storyline that follows. This prologue material is neither redemptive nor progressive in nature. As a matter of fact, as Moses tells the story, the movement of the drama becomes both regressive and somber. If the next stage of history was not somewhat familiar to us, we would be wondering, "Is there any hope for the world?"

Try to think about this soon to unfold drama as if you have never heard it told before. The questions would be endless and the suspense overwhelming. I have a friend who has been working in a mission endeavor in Africa for over twenty years. For many of those years, he and his wife served in a ministry to the Maasai tribe of East Africa. He spent much of his life sharing the gospel of Christ with these semi-nomadic people. His goal in sharing the gospel, however, was not simply to present a typical four-point gospel message about God, man, Christ, and the response. He engaged in what he calls "Bible storying." Instead, he tells the Maasai about how the Bible story unfolds so that they can understand that God is actively working in his world and that he has a plan that includes even them. And, of course, that plan is Christ! He once told me that using the story-telling approach to the gospel means that his Maasai audience has to wait a long time to fully understand the gospel story. At the same time, however, they are being both evangelized and discipled. I write about this mission ministry because I want us to imagine what it would be like if we were a member of the Maasai tribe listening to the Bible story being told in chronological order for the very first time. We would hardly be able to wait for the next chapter of the book. One has to wonder if we could actually put the book down! The prologue has presented us anew with that question—"What is going to happen to the God-forsaken (and God-forsaking) world of Genesis chapters 1–11? Is there any hope? Will matters become worse or get better? Will God do anything? My supposition is that you likely already know some of the answers to those penetrating questions. Nevertheless, I hope that you will continue to read on as if you are a member of this tribe, as one who does not know the story, or simply as someone who has never heard the Bible story before.

Scene One

Step One

The Seed Promise

As we look back at the prologue of the story, we recognize that a great dilemma has been presented. The world is not what it should be. Will God act in a favorable manner? Or will he continue to judge his wayward creatures in some just and righteous fashion? However, grace is about to abound. At the end of Genesis 11 we see a man and his wife, Abram and Sarai, as the Lord (Yahweh) calls out to Abram. Here is the account of the encounter:

> Now the Lord said to Abram, "Go from your country and your kindred and your father's house to the land that I will show you. And I will make of you a great nation, and I will bless you and make your name great, so that you will be a blessing. I will bless those who bless you, and him who dishonors you I will curse, and in you all the families of the earth shall be blessed." (Gen 12:1–3)

One thing should be noted here. According to the text, God is changing his focus. Those early chapters of Genesis display God's working with the *world*. The remainder of Genesis will spotlight God's work with specific *individuals*. If we wish to summarize Genesis chapters 12–50, we simply need to say, "Abraham, Isaac, Jacob, and Joseph." Moses is now addressing God's call to Abram (known eventually as Abraham). He will describe some key events in Abram's life. Please recognize that the story of Abraham is not a biography. It consists of only a handful of pivotal episodes. If we wanted to publish the story of Abraham based on the passages contained in Genesis, his biography would be far too weak and seemingly too silly to publish. The short accounts are all we need to know. They are selective history highlighting God's work with Abraham. Just consider what you would think if I were to tell you the story of my life with just a few points and short stories. Rod was born in Greenville, South Carolina. Rod grew up in Greenville. Rod went to college in Columbia, South Carolina where he became a Christian. Rod met his wife while in seminary and got married at age twenty-four. Rod and his wife had four children. Rod and his wife have lived in Columbia, South Carolina, Gainesville, Florida, Clearwater, Florida and Charlotte, North Carolina; the end! Would you know me? Would those highlighted life events be considered my biography? Of course not! They are simply highlights and very limited ones at that.

So, God comes and he speaks. He takes the initiative. Theologians call this "grace"! God intervenes when mankind has no hope. And when God speaks to Abram, he provides "the seed" necessary to begin his progressive plan of redemption. The seed is a promise and quite the promise it is! This seed is the embryonic promise that will germinate, grow, and blossom throughout the entire world! In this seed, God makes six different promises. We will focus on two in particular (highlighted below in italics) because they summarize everything else in the Bible.

- *I will make of you a great nation*
- I will bless you
- I will make your name great, so that you will be a blessing
- I will bless those who bless you
- Him who dishonors you I will curse
- *In you all the families of the earth shall be blessed*

God tells Abram that he will take him and do two things. Firstly, he will make a great nation of him and from him. This unfolding promise comprises scene one of act one. Act one runs from Genesis chapter 12 through the end of the books of 2 Kings and 2 Chronicles. Secondly, God promises that all of the earth will be blessed through Abram. This unfolding promise comprises act two (the second volume in this series) and will eventually lead us to the goal: "All the earth shall be filled with the knowledge of the glory of God."

What do we need in order to start a nation from one man? First, we need a wife for the man. Abram has one and her name is Sarai. However, there is one problem, a frequent one in this narrative of progress. Sarai is barren; she has never had a child (Gen 11:30). We might also add that Sarai is quite old. To make a nation, God chooses *one* man with a *barren* wife! Why? Because God said, "*I will* do this!" (Gen 21:1). History is God working. When God gives the "seed promise" to Abram, he is seventy-five years old. Abram waits and waits and waits. After eleven years of waiting, Sarai suggests that Abram take her Egyptian servant, Hagar, and have a child through her. Abram is now eighty-six years old. Galatians 4:21–31 tells us that this was an effort of the flesh (or human works), and that Hagar's son Ishmael is not the son of the promise. Abram, therefore, continues to wait. In Genesis 17, he is still waiting and has done so for almost twenty-five years; he is ninety-nine years old. He has been given reminders of the promise (covenant) twice, in Genesis 15 and again in Genesis 17.

Genesis 21:1–2 is, in many ways, the climax to Abraham's story. "The Lord visited Sarah as he had said, and the Lord did to Sarah as he had promised. And Sarah conceived and bore Abraham a son in his old age at the time of which God had spoken to him." At the age of one hundred, along with a wife who is at least ninety years old, the child of the promise enters the world! It is unbelievable! When I was a boy growing up, my home state of South Carolina had a senator who served in public office for close to seventy years, including as a state senator for almost fifty. His name was Strom Thurmond. When he was sixty-six years old, he surprised the state by marrying a former Miss South Carolina, who was only twenty-two years old on their wedding day. At the age of sixty-eight, he shocked the state as his wife gave birth to their first child. Everyone made jokes about his virility, but Senator Thurmond had the last laugh when he and his wife added three more natural children to the fold. The fact that Thurmond could father children at such an advanced age was both improbable and doubtful. Yet it was not impossible and the record shows that it did happen. However, for Abraham at age one hundred, and his wife Sarah at age ninety, to conceive a child was, quite frankly, impossible. Impossible, except for the reality that God had promised such and was able. He could give his word and he has the power and ability to do miracles. Thus, a son is born. Remember the words, "I will!" They are words of promise.

Naturally, we are led to ask the question: "Is this progress?" Yes—finally we see progress. We are celebrating this event like Pentecostals! We are excited and we should be! The Lord has been gracious. The promise is fulfilled and a son named Isaac is born. 1+1=2! *That* is progress. Is this birth the fulfillment of the promise that Abraham will be a great nation? No, but it is the seed of a nation. However, immediately (it seems, although many years have passed) Genesis 22 poses us with an unlikely scenario. God asks Abraham to sacrifice his one and only son, now grown and mature (probably not a young boy). It appears that the years of waiting for progress are about to terminate in one stunning event. 1+1=2-1=1. But God is testing Abraham. God is asking him, "Who do you love more—me or the son of the promise? Do you love the hope of bearing a nation more than me?" Abraham proves both his love for and his faith in the Lord with his willingness to give up his son. God provides a substitute sacrifice. We continue with the two—father and son—remaining alive. But in Genesis 23 we are told that Sarah dies at the age of 127. There will be no other "children of promise." The story now shifts to the son, Isaac, child of the promise.

Genesis 24 is a very unique and lengthy chapter. Abraham gives specific instructions regarding the search for a wife for Isaac. I once heard a sermon by Dr. Charles Stanley in which he said, "God gave us thirty-one verses explaining creation and sixty-seven verses for 'how to find a wife.'" Getting the right wife must be very important! The chapter tells us that Isaac does obtain a wife from Abraham's relatives: Rebekah. Once she is procured, the scene shifts in Genesis 25. In verse 8, we are told that Abraham dies at the age of one hundred seventy-five. We have fourteen chapters in the book of Genesis describing his life, most of which covers around one hundred years of his existence. Seventy-five years and he has only one son and no nation. Now he is gone, and 1+1=2-1=1! Is this progress? The answer must be "yes" because Abraham does have a child of the promise. But God's progress can be very, very slow. We must learn to practice patience when it comes to the plan of God! We wonder—when will the next child appear?

In Genesis 25:21, we see a familiar setting. The woman who needs to give birth in order for the Abrahamic line to continue is . . . barren! Rebekah was sought after and found by Abraham's servant, but she was ultimately chosen by God. God loves to choose and use barren women in his plan because he is the "I will" of the plan. When we can't, he does! God has Isaac right where he wants him. Isaac prays and prays (25:21) and twenty years later (25:26) Rebekah conceives twins who have struggled in her womb. She gives birth to Esau and to Jacob. The two sons—not one—truly appear to be a sign of the blessing of God, as well as a progression toward the goal of a nation. Yet, we discover from both Malachi 1:2–3 and Romans 9:13 that God rejects Esau: "Yet I have loved Jacob but Esau I have hated." Esau despised his birthright and God rejects him from the line of the promise, even though he is the first born. We go from 1+2=3 to 1+1=2. At times, progress in God's program is indeed slow. We must note, however, that God appears to Isaac and repeats the promise originally made to Abraham. Genesis 26:4 states, "I will multiply your offspring as the stars of heaven and will give to your offspring all these lands. And in your offspring all the nations of the earth shall be blessed . . ." The seed promise occurs a second time, this time to Isaac.

In Genesis 28 two significant events occur. Firstly, Jacob is told to get a wife from his own people. He ends up having two wives, Leah, and her younger sister whom he truly loves, Rachel. Secondly, God appears to him in a dream and repeats the "seed promise" to him as well: "Your offspring shall be like the dust of the earth, and you shall spread abroad to the west and to the east and to the north and to the south, and in you and your offspring shall *all* the families of the earth be blessed. Behold, I am with you and will keep you wherever you go, and will bring you back to this land" (Gen 28:14–15, emphasis mine). In Genesis 32, Jacob wrestles with God and his name is changed to Israel. Isaac will live for some years after this and Abraham, Isaac, and Jacob/Israel will all be alive together for a very short period of time. Nevertheless, these three men's stories are told in the book of Genesis as three individual narratives dealing with the same topic: the promise. God gives his promise to each of these men, assuring each one that they will become a great nation, and that God will bless the entire world through their posterity. These three men are thus to be known as the patriarchs, the founders, the forefathers of Israel. Together, as bearers of the promise, they are the original seed that will become a nation and provide blessing to the world. Their stories are simply generational photos. Each receives the promise and each is called to trust God to keep his promise. Nowhere in the Bible does God say, "I am the God of Adam, Seth, or Enoch." Constantly in the Bible, God is referred to as the "God of Abraham, Isaac, and Jacob."[1] 1+1+1=1! The one promise is more important than the men to whom it was made. These three receive the seed of the promise that will germinate into a vast people of God, innumerable like the grains of sand on the seashore, or the stars illuminating the heavens. This seed—the promise to Abraham, Isaac, and Jacob—is the beginning of the redemptive program of God! This seed is step one in God's progress of redemption.

"He is the LORD our God; his judgments are in all the earth. [8] He remembers his covenant forever, the word that he commanded,

---

1. See Genesis 32:9, 50:24; Exodus 2:24, 3:6, 15, 16, 4:5, 6:3, 8, 33:1; Leviticus 26:42; Deuteronomy 1:8, 9:5, 30:20, etc.

for a thousand generations, ⁹ the covenant that he made with Abraham, his sworn promise to Isaac, ¹⁰ which he confirmed to Jacob as a statute, to Israel as an everlasting covenant, ¹¹ saying, 'To you I will give the land of Canaan as your portion for an inheritance.'" (Ps 105:7–11)

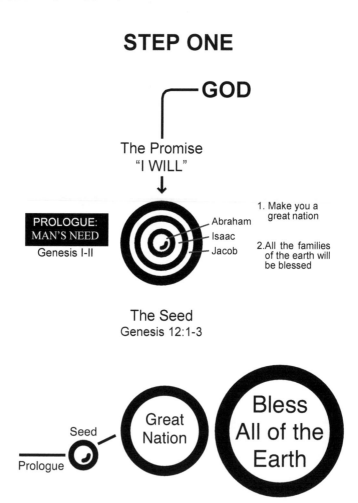

STEP ONE

GOD

The Promise
"I WILL"

PROLOGUE:
MAN'S NEED
Genesis I-II

Abraham
Isaac
Jacob

1. Make you a great nation

2. All the families of the earth will be blessed

The Seed
Genesis 12:1-3

Seed
Prologue

Great Nation

Bless All of the Earth

THE GOAL:
"ALL THE EARTH SHALL BE FILLED WITH THE KNOWLEDGE OF THE GLORY OF GOD!" (HABAKKUK 2:14)

Scene One

Step Two

The Twelve Tribes

WE NOW TURN OUR attention to Genesis chapter 29. In verse 31, we find the predictable descriptor of Jacob's wife, Rachel: she is barren. By now, we are not surprised, but once again, we are left to wonder, "What will God do?" The text tells us that the Lord opened the womb of Jacob's first—and unloved—wife, Leah. Jacob has his first son and names him Reuben. Notice what happens in the next few verses and through the end of the chapter. Not much is noted, except that sons are born on a regular basis, including through two wives, who battle via their female servants. Here is the list:

1. Reuben (Gen 29:31–32)—through Leah
2. Simeon (Gen 29:33)—through Leah
3. Levi (Gen 29:34)—through Leah
4. Judah (Gen 29:35)—through Leah

A cursory read of the text almost makes it sound as though Leah has had *four sons in four days*! Again, this is selective history; the most important matter being that Israel is multiplying. The births continue in the following chapter:

5. Dan (Gen 30:1–6)—through Rachel's servant Bilhah
6. Naphtali (Gen 30:7)—through Rachel's servant Bilhah
7. Gad (Gen 30:9–11)—through Leah's servant Zilpah

8. Asher (Gen 30:12–13)—through Leah's servant Zilpah

9. Issachar (Gen 30:17–18)—through Leah

10. Zebulun (Gen 30:19–20)—through Leah

11. Joseph (Gen 30:22–24)—through Rachel (her first)

12. Benjamin—mentioned later in Genesis 35:18, born to Rachel, who dies in childbirth

Some observations should be made about this "progress." Rachel's servant gives birth to Dan, but Dan is received as a son, unlike Ishmael, who was born to Sarah's servant. God receives Dan and the other sons born by Jacob's wives' servants. No reason is given for their reception in the redemptive plan; they are simply included in and chosen for God's plan. God's ways are higher than our ways!

The birth of these twelve sons is step two in scene one of the redemptive plan. Step one was 1+1+1=1 ("the seed"). In step two, we suddenly (it seems) have twelve sons! Do we now have a nation? Not quite! Just as step one was a seed with the potential for a nation, so step two contains twelve seeds with potential for that nation. In Ruth 4:11, we find these words, "May the LORD make the woman, who is coming into your house, like Rachel and Leah, who together built up the house of Israel." This is the legacy of Rachel and Leah—they provided the sons who would be the seeds of the twelve tribes of Israel (Gen 49:28). The nation of Israel would be unified and known by the twelve tribes. The twelve sons would be seen as the "tribal chiefs," the heads, and/or the progenitors of the tribes, and in essence, the future nation of Israel.

The progress is slow. We would say that this progress was very slow. In step one, we ultimately have only one seed consisting of the one promise made to the three patriarchs. Together, Abraham, Isaac, and Jacob represent that one seed. But in step two, we now have twelve seeds. These twelve are the seeds for the tribes that will eventually become the nation of Israel. Genesis 46:27 tells us that the twelve tribes eventually consist of seventy people. The progress begins small, but we are able to watch it grow. Is *this* progress? Definitely, yes! 1+12=70.

STEP TWO

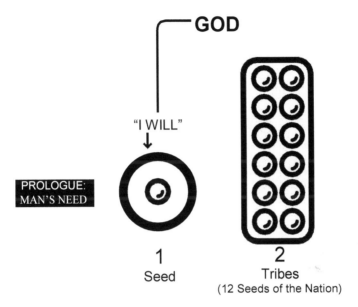

1
Seed

2
Tribes
(12 Seeds of the Nation)

Joseph

From the three patriarchs who represent one seed, to the twelve sons of Jacob who represent the twelve tribes (or twelve seeds) and the future of Israel, the book of Genesis turns its attention to one of the sons of Jacob—probably the most famous son of Jacob—for a number of reasons. Moses spends a considerable amount of time—fourteen chapters—telling the story of Joseph (Gen 37–50). This is a lot of material, so Joseph must be a very important figure. We will not recount his story, except to summarize it. Joseph is Jacob's favorite son. His jealous brothers sell him to a travelling caravan that leads him to Egypt. Through many trials, temptations, and a series of providential circumstances, he becomes the second most powerful man in Egypt. A famine occurs bringing his family (Jacob, his sons, and their families, totaling seventy persons in all, according to Genesis 46:27) to Egypt where, ultimately, they are reunited at Pharaoh's palace.

So, why Joseph? God never says, "I am the God of Joseph!" Joseph is significant because through him the potential nation of Israel, as seen in the twelve tribes, is kept safe. Joseph's role in God's plan of redemption is singular in its focus—he prevents the extinction of God's people. Because the people of Israel were shepherds, Pharaoh provides the land of Goshen that they might keep their sheep there (shepherds were odious to Egyptians). This land was the best of the land, the best of Rameses. This small band of people—the twelve tribes and their families—are given the protection of Pharaoh, king of Egypt. Joseph serves as what I call the "protective umbrella," providing safety for God's people.

We could well assume that had they remained in the Promised Land (Canaan), they would have been endangered by two possible threats. Firstly by annihilation—these seventy people were so limited in number that they could have easily been killed and destroyed by the surrounding pagan nations in Canaan, a land filled with godless barbarians. Obliteration was a distinct possibility, especially as the tribes would grow and become a looming enemy of the pagans in the land. Secondly by assimilation, or accommodation—sadly, it is often the norm for God's people to adopt the ways and morals (or lack of morals) of the surrounding culture. The surrounding nations in Canaan were so evil that God has to move his people to a much culturally safer place. For Israel, potentially, their life in Canaan would be like a westerner living in the midst of ISIS in the twenty-first century. God had earlier told Abraham that this move would be necessary when he stated in Genesis 15:16, "And they shall come back here in the fourth generation, for the iniquity of the Amorites is not yet complete." The people of Israel are small and are thus transplanted to a place where they can thrive, i.e., the nation of Egypt. This move is the reason for Joseph's story and Joseph himself seems to understand it when, in Genesis 45: 4–7, he reunites with his brothers,

> [4] So Joseph said to his brothers, "Come near to me, please." And they came near. And he said, "I am your brother, Joseph, whom you sold into Egypt. [5] And now do not be distressed or angry with yourselves because you sold me here, for God sent me before you to preserve life. [6] For the famine has been in the land these two years, and there are yet five years in which there will be neither plowing nor harvest. [7] *And God sent me before you to preserve for you a remnant on earth, and to keep alive for you many survivors.* (Italics mine for emphasis)

Furthermore, Joseph recognizes the good hand of God in the lives of both himself and his family when he declares the profound statement regarding

God's providence, "As for you, you meant evil against me, but God meant it for good, to bring it about that many people should be kept alive, as they are today" (Gen 50:20). Is this progress? Technically, no. There is no growth among the people of God; they are simply transferred from one land to another. But they are protected from debilitating influences and sent to an environment where they can safely thrive. Joseph leads us to step three.

JOSEPH

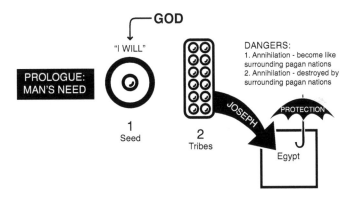

Scene One

Step Three

A Multitude

As we think about the promise made to Abraham, Isaac, and Jacob, we must ask this question, "What do we need to have a nation?" The answers are multiple in nature. The components of a nation are a land, a people, a culture, and a leader (though a more technical answer would be territory, population, government, and sovereignty). As we move forward in God's progress, we will watch as the Lord brings together these various elements. Step three involves the growth of a mass of people thriving in suitable soil for multiplication!

When I was a college student at the University of South Carolina in the 1970s, my major required that I take an introductory course in microbiology. There were two professors for a particular Microbiology 101 course, one as droll and lifeless as possibly could be, and another whom we were told was lively and could entertain students about the subject for the entire semester. My professor, sad to say, was indeed Dr. Monotone, and I remember very little, if anything, he said. But what I do remember stems from the lab that was required to supplement the course. My most vibrant memory—and an image that still resides in my mind to this day—was the lab experiment that we were required to do with the Staphylococcus Epidermidis bacteria (commonly known as staph). We were told that staph lives on our fingers (our skin) and for the experiment we would have to place a finger print inside a fresh, new, pristine petri dish containing agar (the growth substance or the "culture" in scientific terms). Then we would return the next week to see what happened. One week is a long time for an experiment to work, but I still recall returning to the biology building on Main Street to look into a sanitized glass case holding all of our labeled petri dishes. Mine had grown immensely, as had many others. We had provided the perfect environment for a successful experiment. One student had accidentally left his petri dish cover open and his staph was running all over the outside of the dish, an awful greyish and whitish hairball-looking overflow. Ugh! But one thing was certain. Staph placed in a healthy petri dish designed for its growth had flourished!

This scientific story is written with a purpose and brings us to step three which is found in the first chapter of Exodus. We must remember that the historical books of the Bible do not provide us with a complete history. In Exodus 1:1–5, we are given a summary of the events that occurred at the end of Genesis. This is year one in Egypt:

> These are the names of the sons of Israel who came to Egypt with Jacob, each with his household: [2] Reuben, Simeon, Levi, and Judah, [3] Issachar, Zebulun, and Benjamin, [4] Dan and Naphtali, Gad and Asher. [5] All the descendants of Jacob were seventy persons; Joseph was already in Egypt.

This is a depiction of a "baby nation." This description is neither of a seed, nor of a nation. In Exodus 1:6, however, we are given an eleven-word description summarizing an unspecified time in Israel's history. Moses writes, "Then Joseph died, and all his brothers and all that generation." It appears that the baby nation is gone. However, in the next verse, Moses lets us know what happens following the aforementioned death of the tribal fathers, a period covering a few hundred years, with some surmising that it was approximately three hundred and fifty.[1] This is one of those huge gaps in history that we find in the Scriptures. It is a long yawn in time, one in which we might expect more details. In a few hundred years, nothing else significant has transpired except for this one thing. In one verse, Exodus 1:7, we are told that an amazing phenomenon has occurred, "But the people of Israel were *fruitful* and *increased greatly*; they *multiplied* and grew *exceedingly strong*, so that the land was *filled* with them" (italics mine for emphasis). In one verse, the need for people to create a nation is described as fulfilled! This is one productive verse! The land of Goshen has been an effective petri

---

1. Exodus 12:40 mentions that the people of Israel lived in Egypt for four hundred and thirty years. If we include the years that the patriarchs, Jacob and his family live there, we can estimate that Exodus 1:7 describes a period of time that covers over three centuries.

dish for the people of God. The women are fertile. Babies are everywhere. The people are abundant and the land is filled with them. Moses gives an accurate summary statement of what happened in the petri dish of Egypt when he writes, "And you shall make response before the LORD your God, 'A wandering Aramean was my father. And he went down into Egypt and sojourned there, few in number, and there he became a nation, great, mighty, and populous.'" (Deut 26:5).

Moses uses a few brief stories and his own biography as examples of God's prevailing providence over the Egyptians. Moses wants his audience, the Israelites, to recognize that when God is working, Satan is always opposing that work. The first story describes what we might call opposition number one. In Exodus 1:8–11 we are told that the Egyptians become concerned about the growth of the Israelite slaves and so begin to oppress them with taskmasters and heavy burdens. But as the text continues, we discover that the more the people of God are oppressed, the more they multiply. This makes the Egyptians dread the Israelites, which by implication, suggests that they dread the God of the Israelites! So, the Egyptians made every effort to make the Israelites' lives bitter, treating them ruthlessly. However, the worse the Israelites are treated and the harder they are worked, the more they grow! I can only imagine what the end of the work day looked like for the average Israelite slave when he returns home and finishes his evening meal: "Honey, let's go for a walk in the neighborhood . . . " "Dear, would you like to play some Scrabble tonight after dinner?" "Let's just kick back and watch some television!" I rather imagine that with long days and short nights, populating the nation was probably the activity that prevailed on the home front. And although that thought is a bit humorous, Exodus 1:12–14 is quite explicit that the more vigorously they were worked, the more vigorously they reproduced. God's progress *will* prevail!

The next story describes opposition number two. In brief, the king of Egypt instructs the midwives who assist in the birth of slave children, to kill the babies if their gender is male. This edict is a directive to participate in a post-partum murder. But the midwives fear God and permit the boys to live. The text is conclusive: "So God dealt well with the midwives. And the people *multiplied* and *grew very strong*" (Exod 1:20, italics mine for emphasis). The Israelites continue to multiply and increase, growing ever larger. God's will cannot be thwarted! Opposition number three involves Pharaoh's instructions regarding the boys who survive birth and by implication, those who survive the edict directed toward their immediate murders at birth. The

34

command is issued to all of the people, stating that every Israelite boy born (or found) must be thrown into the river to be drowned.

The conclusion to scene one/step three is that a multitude of people have arisen by the hand of God in the midst of great opposition. The fact that the multiplying Israelites are so odious to the Egyptians serves the purpose of preventing cultural diffusion among God's people. The cultural assimilation that could have occurred among the small band of Jacob's twelve tribes while living in Canaan, within arm's reach of the Amorites, will never occur among this growing, thriving people of God. The fact that they are being oppressed by their domineering tyrants, the Egyptians, will prevent it. Not only have they increased in number, but their identity as enslaved and oppressed Israelites brings a sense of corporate unity among God's people.

The God who made the promise to Abraham has made the seed flourish in Egypt. The protective umbrella provided by Joseph's providentially designed enslavement (including his brothers' jealousy and hatred) has borne the fruit of proliferation! We now see a great multitude of people comprising the nation of Israel, united under the suffering of their oppressors. They are huge, possibly two million strong. Is this progress? It is progress beyond our imagination. The Maasai tribe would be stunned and amazed to hear this step of the story.

STEP THREE

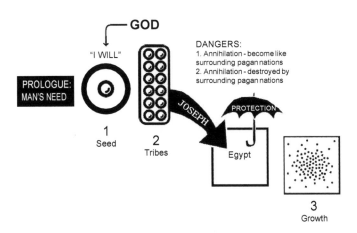

Scene One

Step Four

The Leader

THE SECOND CHAPTER OF Exodus involves a distinct shift in the nature of the historical material presented by Moses. In chapter 1, the book of Exodus focuses upon the significant growth of God's people, with hundreds of thousands being added despite opposition within a matter of a few verses. Do we have a nation? Yes—and no! We do have a multitude of people who are united in their uniform suffering. But we need more. We need a leader. And God is about to raise up one for his people. Exodus 2:1–10 provides a meager summary of the following: this leader's birth, his providential deliverance from potential death by the edict of Pharaoh, King of Egypt, and his growth into manhood. Much like the childhood accounts of Christ, we are not told much about his childhood and upbringing.

However, Exodus 2:11, tells us that when this leader named Moses has grown up (forty years old, according to Acts 7:23), he visits his fellow Hebrews in order to view their dilemma and the distress of their slavery. The text assumes that he knows who he is in his heritage as a true Israelite; we can only imagine that his mother gave him many history lessons about the people of God. Thinking that he can deliver the enslaved Israelites himself, Moses kills an Egyptian taskmaster who is beating a fellow Hebrew. Apparently, Moses believes that he can be the ruler, deliverer, and judge for his people, but he has not yet learned the ways of God. Having been discovered by his own people and also by Pharaoh, Moses flees southeast into the desert area of Midian. As we observe Moses's flight, we must ask the inevitable question: "Is this progress?" The entire scene appears to be action going in the wrong direction.

In Midian, Moses marries (Zipporah) and becomes a sheep herder, laboring for his father-in-law, Jethro. He spends forty years tending sheep and it appears he is wasting away far from home and with very little purpose. Yet, it is in this role that God prepares him to eventually tend the sheep that are God's people. I once heard Old Testament scholar Dr. Walt Kaiser say that Moses had to spend forty years listening to sheep bleating "baa . . . baa" because he would spend the next forty years listening to God's people in the wilderness bleating "manna . . . manna"! God's training program was perfect for this future leader of his people.

While tending the sheep near Mount Horeb, Moses is called by God in a most unusual fashion. A burning bush that is not consumed draws his attention and the narrative tells us what happens next,

> When the LORD saw that he turned aside to see, God called to him out of the bush, "Moses, Moses!" And he said, "Here I am." [5] Then he said, "Do not come near; take your sandals off your feet, for the place on which you are standing is holy ground." [6] And he said, "I am the God of your father, the God of Abraham, the God of Isaac, and the God of Jacob." And Moses hid his face, for he was afraid to look at God. (Exod 3:4–6)

God then tells Moses that he has seen the suffering of his people ". . . and I have come down to deliver them out of the hand of the Egyptians and to bring them up out of that land to a good and broad land, a land flowing with milk and honey . . ." (Exod 3:8). The call is clear—God is going to deliver his people. Yet, in Exodus 3:10 the Lord says, "Come, I will send you to Pharaoh that you may bring my people, the children of Israel, out of Egypt." There appears to be a contradiction regarding the nature of Israel's leader! In verse 8, we see that God himself will lead them, but in verse 10, it seems that Moses is responsible to lead them.[1] However, this seeming contradiction is resolved by understanding the nature of God's leadership. God leads his people through the man of his choice! This leadership style is a picture of the type of nation that God is going to build—a theocracy! A theocracy is a nation of people who serve the living God, following a leader

---

1. In a rather humorous fashion, we see these two roles, i.e., God leading and Moses leading, pitted against each other in Exodus 32:7 and 11, where neither God nor Moses will claim the people as their own after the incident of golden calf idolatry. They turn to each other and call the people of Israel "your people!"

who serves both God and his people. Moses is that leader! Leadership selection is step four in God's drama of redemption—the choice of the man to lead the masses out of their condition and habitation of slavery.

STEP FOUR

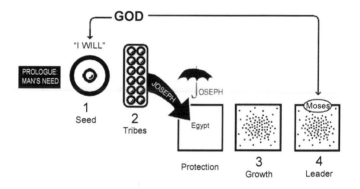

Scene One

Step Five

"Out"

WE NOW HAVE BOTH a leader and a nation of people. What is next? First, the Lord has to assure Moses that as the great "I AM" he is powerful enough to deliver the captive Hebrews from Egypt, and can use Moses in the endeavor. Then he sends Moses and his brother Aaron, whom the Lord has recruited to help Moses, to appear before Pharaoh and make one simple request: "Thus says the LORD, the God of Israel, 'Let my people go . . .'" (Exod 5:1). To paraphrase Moses's request, we might say, "King, we would like to slip out of the country!" Pharaoh is quite perturbed at the request and replies, "Who is the LORD . . . ?" (Exod 5:2). Had Moses known exactly what was going to happen, he would have replied, "Pharaoh, I wish you hadn't asked that question!" The Lord will answer Pharaoh's inquiry with ten special demonstrations of his power that Pharaoh will never forget![1]

The problem that must be faced in the present situation is that, despite their slavery, the Israelites are their own nation. And it is a sociological principle that one nation cannot exist within another nation, and certainly not on the land of that nation. Looking back at Israel's past, Moses himself states, "Or has any god ever attempted to go and *take a nation for himself from the midst of another nation*, by trials, by signs, by wonders, and by war, by a mighty hand and an outstretched arm, and by great deeds of terror,

---

1. I have written a song to the tune of Paul Simon's 1975 hit song, "Fifty Ways to Leave Your Lover," but entitled it "Ten Sure Ways to Leave Your Pharaoh." The lyrics of my song, which are far more biblical than Simon's, are provided below as Appendix One.

all of which the LORD your God did for you in Egypt before your eyes?" (Deut 4:34, italics mine). The people of God, as a nation, must depart from the nation to whom they are enslaved. The benefit (i.e., massive population growth) of the protective umbrella of Egypt provided by Joseph's enslavement has passed and they need to be delivered. They need salvation!

The means of this deliverance is quite unusual. If we were to ask leaders of a powerful nation such as America today to deliver these captives, surely they would send in multiple stealth bombers, thousands of Marine troops, or some advanced military means of power. But, shockingly, the Lord God simply uses sprinkled blood and faith as the means to deliver his people from Egypt. Salvation is of the Lord! In later passages, the Lord declares this refrain, "I am the LORD your God, who brought you out of the land of Egypt . . ." (Num 15:41, Deut 5:6, as a preface to the Ten Commandments, and 2 Kgs 17:36, among others). This deliverance is not procured by man, but only by God and only in God's way!

Moses gives his summary of the deliverance of God's people in two passages. The first passage describes the Passover, or the deliverance of God's people by both sprinkled blood and faith:

> The time that the people of Israel lived in Egypt was 430 years. [41] At the end of 430 years, on that very day, all the hosts of the LORD went out from the land of Egypt. [42] It was a night of watching by the LORD, to bring them out of the land of Egypt; so this same night is a night of watching kept to the LORD by all the people of Israel throughout their generations. [43] And the LORD said to Moses and Aaron, "This is the statute of the Passover . . . " (Exod 12:40-42)

The Passover is the greatest demonstration of God's sovereign and elective power yet seen and typifies the shed blood of Christ on the cross centuries later. Israel is the chosen people who are delivered by faith, through the means of sprinkled blood by a Savior they cannot see, but must fully trust. And their evil captors, typifying Satan's enslavement over those living in darkness apart from God, are painfully and woefully judged. The Israelites demonstrate their faith by placing the blood of a slain lamb on the sides (doorposts) and top ("lintel") of the entrances to their homes (a picture of the cross), while the Egyptians are judged due to both the absence of a lamb's blood slain on their behalf and the faith that must trust it for deliverance from God's judgment.

The second passage describes the escape from Pharaoh's army when the Israelites walk across a fully dried Red Sea and look back to see their close pursuers put to death.

> The waters returned and covered the chariots and the horsemen; of all the host of Pharaoh that had followed them into the sea, not one of them remained. [29] But the people of Israel walked on dry ground through the sea, the waters being a wall to them on their right hand and on their left. [30] Thus the LORD saved Israel that day from the hand of the Egyptians, and Israel saw the Egyptians dead on the seashore. [31] Israel saw the great power that the LORD used against the Egyptians, so the people feared the LORD, and they believed in the LORD and in his servant Moses. (Exod 14:28–31)

In the crossing of the Red Sea, the people of God are enabled to actually observe the great power of God on display. Buck Hatch says that the miracle of the parting of the Red Sea is probably the greatest demonstration of God's power in history until the resurrection of his Son.

Now, we must ask two questions. First, is this progress? Yes, this is progress—the people of God are moving, as a nation, into freedom. Second, is it now time for the people of Israel to enter the Promised Land, the land of Canaan? Yes and no—they are almost ready, but we need one more step, and it is an essential one.

STEP FIVE

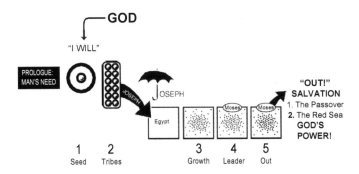

Scene One

Step Six

Culture

THE NATION OF ISRAEL is now free from their captors, wonderfully liberated by the Lord God, and following their leader, Moses. Thus, they appear ready to enter the land. But we experience a pause in their journey as they come to a grinding halt for one year at Mount Sinai. They stop in order to hear from God and to gain their proper identity as his people. From Exodus 19 through the book of Deuteronomy, rather than history, we see primarily discourse and instruction. I have built a solid premise that the unity of the Scriptures is found in history and thus far we have been looking, in survey fashion, at narrative material. Nevertheless, although step six is primarily "God speaking" rather than "God acting," we recognize that, as they move toward the Promised Land, the nation of Israel needs a defined *culture* in order to survive. Their culture is given to them by spoken revelation from their divine leader; this revelation we know as the "Law." The Law of God is summarized in three major categories: 1) the moral law, or the Ten Commandments, found in Exodus 20; 2) the ceremonial law, or the way to worship God and the means for becoming right with God; and 3) the civil law, or the way to live as the people of God in relation to one another in his nation. The bottom line is that these prescribed laws, otherwise seen as the mandated culture of God's people, has a necessary purpose. They prevent a multitude from becoming a mob!

STEP SIX

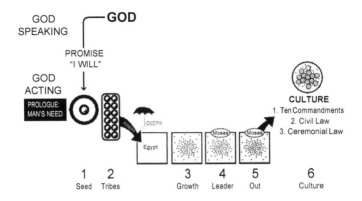

Scene One

The Challenge

Failure

PEOPLE, LEADER, AND CULTURE. The obvious conclusion is that the nation of Israel is ready to enter the Promised Land. We can only imagine the anticipation both on an individual and corporate level. Numbers 13–14 give us a dramatic account of the plan to search out the land of Canaan. If we read through the first twenty-five verses of chapter 13, we will discover eight references either to "the land" or to "Canaan." The people are fixated with the thought of the land. They will soon be faced with a challenge of courage!

In Numbers 13, the Lord tells Moses to explore the land he is *giving* to them. Moses creates a wise military strategy and provides a plan to spy out the land. Giving the land is God's part; exploring the land is man's part. Leaders are chosen—not the fainthearted—but trusted, reliable, proven men from each tribe (as a means of preventing bias or jealousy). Their task, as spies, is to do a demographic study—to assess a few characteristics of the land: the people, the population, the towns and their fortifications, the soil and the fruit (Num 13:17-20). They spend forty days of diligent spying (probably split into teams), during the hot time of the year when the grapes would be ripe. Theirs was a very dangerous task. Surely, the people were waiting in suspense during those long forty days. I'm certain that their imaginations were running wild with steady impatience and enormous anticipation. I think of my time as a college student at the University of South Carolina, when a friend and classmate of mine invited me to go on a blind date with him, his girlfriend, and her roommate. Every night that week (and it seemed like an extraordinarily long week), I dreamed about what my prospective date would look like and be like. I can only wonder what the Israelites were dreaming about during those forty days of exploration. (And for the curious, she was a cute, sweet girl, but I was a bore, so that was that!)

The spies returned, but the reviews were mixed. The challenge of courage was met by three attitudes that paralyzed their (and our) courage. Despite the fact that God had promised them this land, and that there were close to six hundred thousand Israelite soldiers, the majority report by the spies was exceedingly pessimistic. Three negative attitudes prevailed among ten of the twelve explorers. First, there was an attitude of *obstacles*: ". . . We came to the land to which you sent us. It flows with milk and honey, and this is its fruit. However, the people who dwell in the land are strong, and the cities are fortified and very large. And besides, we saw the descendants of Anak there" (Num 13:27–28). They explained the good news about the wonderful resources of the land that awaited them, but then presented bad news: the cities are fortified, the land is filled with the descendants of Anak, a people who are like giants, and the residents of the land are foreign and intimidating.

The first obstacle bothers the masses so much that they allow a second discouraging obstacle to surface: an attitude of *powerlessness*: ". . . We are not able to go up against the people, for they are stronger than we are" (Num 13:31). The people are only able to look at themselves and their own inabilities. Numbers 14:2 describes how the fear and insecurity of the crowd takes over and turns into both mass weeping and such deep grumbling that it spreads like a deadly cancer throughout the body. The people become irrational, wishing they had died in Egypt instead of dying in the desert.

A third and final obstacle is presented when the whole assembly begins to ask the "why" question! In a mood of grumbling, the people express an attitude of *questioning*: "Why is the LORD bringing us into this land, to fall by the sword? Our wives and our little ones will become a prey. Would it not be better for us to go back to Egypt?" (Num 14:3). The words *why* and *better* are key phrases exhibiting their ungodly attitude. We know from many Scriptures that the Lord allows perplexity and questioning from his people when tough times come, but once we conclude that our plan is better than his and fight against him, we have turned our hearts away from both his will and his love. These three obstacles crush the hopes of the people and the Promised Land appears as a false dream.[1]

1. The following are sources of courage that could have sustained the people in the

Ultimately, there are two primary reasons leading to the failure of God's people to enter the land. Joshua addresses the first when he speaks to the frenzied, harried crowd in their distress, "If the LORD delights in us, he will bring us into this land and give it to us, a land that flows with milk and honey. ⁹ Only do not *rebel* against the LORD" (Num 14:8–9, italics mine). This spirit of rebellion and resistance to both the LORD and his leaders has consumed the people in grand fashion. Rebellion against (or disobedience toward) the LORD is one of the most serious sins mentioned in the Bible. The state of the people's hearts will not go unjudged. Secondly, not only is rebellion involved, but the people have lost faith in both the LORD and in his designated leaders. "And the LORD said to Moses, 'How long will this people despise me? And how long will they *not believe* in me, in spite of all the signs that I have done among them?'" (Num 14:11, italics mine). The Israelites have reached the point where they can no longer trust in the Lord. They have lost faith, despite having both seen and experienced his greatness and power in their deliverance from Egypt. Rebellion and unbelief—these are the reactions of God's people after seeing him work previously in tremendous ways. Is this progress? No, there is no progress here. All we are able to observe is an event fully characterized as *failure*! Just like the script on a wayward middle schooler's report card, the big "F" predominates this stage of Israelites' trek out of Egypt and into the Promised Land. Where there should be faith and obedience, there is unbelief and rebellion. And the sad, sad result is that this generation will never enter the Promised Land. Rather, they will wander aimlessly in the desert wilderness for approximately forty years, as they drop off in death, one-by-one, in a place of desolation. Even Moses will fail to enter because he publicly dishonors the Lord. Obstacles prevail over opportunities, and failure is spawned where faith should have grown. This failure seems to be a major setback for the seed promise made to Abraham. The Maasai tribe would be

---

midst of their trial. 1) God's *Promise*: Numbers 13:30 (see verse 2): God has promised the land to the people; he will certainly give it to them. The word *certainly (yacal)* means "to overcome, be victors, succeed, prevail, [and to] endure." 2) God's *Pleasure*: Numbers 14:8: The people can trust God and not rebel against him. The word "pleased" *(chafats)* means "to delight in, have affection toward." It is God's pleasure to bless us as we trust him (see also Hebrews 11:6). 3) God's *Presence*: Numbers 14:9: Caleb and Joshua declare, "God is with us; therefore, do not fear." The minority report believes in the supernatural presence of God to help them. 4) God's *Providence*: Numbers 14:9: The time is right. God will protect them. The word "protection" *(tsal)* speaks of "shade, shadows, defense, [and] walls." Joshua and Caleb believe the words that the Lord spoke to Abraham in Genesis 15:16, that he will judge the pagans in the land when the sin of the Amorites is full. It is now time to watch God conquer his enemies.

wondering, "Will there ever be a God-fearing people living as a nation in the Promised Land?" The Maasai would probably relate to the forthcoming wilderness wanderings as well.

However, in the midst of this dark chapter in Israel's history, there is a silver lining. God is still at work and his plan will not be thwarted, nor will he be prevented from reaching his goal, i.e., the second half of the seed promise made to Abraham, Isaac, and Jacob. Immediately after the devastating setback of national rebellion, and Moses's plea that they might be spared, God makes this astounding declaration, "Then the LORD said, 'I have pardoned, according to your word. ²¹ But truly, as I live, and as *all the earth shall be filled with the glory of the Lord* . . .'" (Num 14:20–21, italics mine for emphasis). When the future looks as bleak as possible, the LORD is still in control. His sovereign will cannot be deterred by the sins of his people. His plan will triumph and his goal of glorifying himself throughout the earth will be accomplished. Failure in the lives of God's people is never the final word!

FAILURE

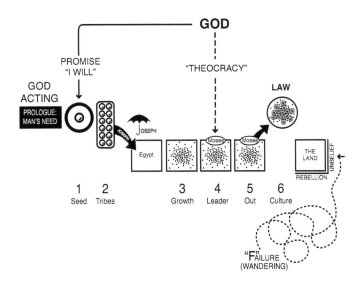

Scene One

Step Seven

The Land

AFTER THE WILDERNESS WANDERING is complete, God speaks to the next generation. This is recorded in the book of Deuteronomy. The name "Deuteronomy" comes from the combination of two words, and means "second law." The law, or culture that was given to this generation's parents prior to the rebellion that prevented them from entering the land, must be repeated to the children who are themselves now grown and ready to enter. Having been properly prepared, it is time to enter the Promised Land. Joshua is a book of "victory," and is therefore very encouraging. We are able to see the Lord work mightily, especially after the massive failure on the part of his people some forty years earlier.

Here are some sample passages demonstrating the victorious nature of the book of Joshua. Firstly:

> For the LORD your God dried up the waters of the Jordan for you until you passed over, as the LORD your God did to the Red Sea, which he dried up for us until we passed over, ²⁴ so that all the peoples of the earth may know that the hand of the LORD is mighty, that you may fear the LORD your God forever. (Josh 4:23–24)

I must mention that many people do not realize that, just as the people of Israel passed through the Red Sea on dry land with Moses while fleeing the Egyptians, they also similarly crossed the river Jordan through the leadership of Joshua. They entered the Promised Land through the miraculous hand of God. What a journey of victory! Secondly, in the middle of the book of Joshua, we read, "There has been no day like it before or since, when the LORD heeded the voice of a man, for the LORD fought for Israel" (Josh 10:14). No matter what the explanation, "the day the sun stood still" was a day like none other on the face of the earth, and was also a testimony to the reality that the Lord God of Israel fights for his people. Lastly, near the end of the book, we read, "Not one word of all the good promises that the LORD had made to the house of Israel had failed; all came to pass" (Josh 21:45). This verse is the summary verse for the entire book of Joshua, testifying that God's hand was upon his people. Although the earlier generation did not believe God's promise to give them the land, and passed away in failure, the next generation was able to see God keep his promises.

The book of Joshua is simply divided into two sections:

- The conquest of the land (chapters 1–12)

- The division or assignment of the land (chapters 13–24)

The first section is summarized in Joshua 10:40–42.

> So Joshua struck the whole land, the hill country and the Negeb and the lowland and the slopes, and all their kings. He left none remaining, but devoted to destruction all that breathed, just as the LORD God of Israel commanded. [41] And Joshua struck them from Kadesh-barnea as far as Gaza, and all the country of Goshen, as far as Gibeon. [42] And Joshua captured all these kings and their land at one time, because the LORD God of Israel fought for Israel. [43] Then Joshua returned, and all Israel with him, to the camp at Gilgal.

Written in the hyperbolic fashion of the ancient near east, we are to understand that Joshua was able to conquer the entire land of Canaan. He has not necessarily made conquest of every single individual, but he has subdued key leadership of the pagan groups who reside there. The army of Israel is breaking the power of local kings living in Canaan. Joshua is proving his authority over the kings and their land, and asserting control of the Promised Land in its entirety. The troops then return to the camp headquarters at Gilgal once the task of conquest is completed.

The second section of the book (chapters 13–24), begins by noting that Joshua is ageing in both his life and leadership, so the Lord lays out the portions of the land that remain to be conquered (13:1–2). Then Joshua is instructed to divide the land into allotments for the various tribes of Israel, "Now therefore divide this land for an inheritance to the nine tribes and half the tribe of Manasseh" (13:7). Chapters 13 and beyond (through chapter 19) provide the dimensions of the divided land for the tribes under consideration.[1]

Two significant battles (among others) are highlighted in the section covering the conquest of the land. Those battles include the well-known battle of Jericho and the less recognized battle of Ai. The battle of Jericho is found in Joshua chapters 5 and 6. It is the rarest of battles because it doesn't use men to win the fight. Instead, Joshua and the people are asked to use the most ridiculous strategy conceivable in order to conquer. Joshua describes Israel's command to engage in battle,

> You shall march around the city, all the men of war going around the city once. Thus shall you do for six days. [4] Seven priests shall bear seven trumpets of rams' horns before the ark. On the seventh day you shall march around the city seven times, and the priests shall blow the trumpets. [5] And when they make a long blast with the ram's horn, when you hear the sound of the trumpet, then all the people shall shout with a great shout, and the wall of the city will fall down flat, and the people shall go up, everyone straight before him." (Josh 6:3–5)

With this seemingly bizarre approach to warfare, we wonder what attitude might the Lord be dealing with in this next, younger generation of Israel. Simply stated, he is asking the question, "Can you trust me?" He is addressing their previous problem of unbelief. Unbelief is the problem that occurred at the time Israel failed to enter the Promised Land. God is demonstrating, through a lesson seemingly beyond comprehension, that he does not need anybody to fight his fights! He wants them to remember Jericho when they move forward to fight future fights, as well as when, inevitably, they confront other human enemies in the land. Faith, trust, and belief in the God who fights for them must be their posture when they move forward to live as God's people.

Sadly, however, a ban that was given when the soldiers ransacked fallen Jericho is violated. The Lord God had declared, "But you, keep yourselves from the things devoted to destruction, lest when you have devoted them you take any of the devoted things and make the camp of Israel a thing for destruction and bring trouble upon it" (Josh 6:18). With a victory over Jericho in hand, the Israelites give little consideration to the small town of Ai, as they proceed to send only a small number of troops (three thousand)

---

1. The Reubenites, the Gadites, and half the tribe of Manasseh had previously made known their desire to settle in the land on the east side of the Jordan.

into battle. Joshua 7:1 tells us that the Lord is displeased and angry with the fact that an Israelite soldier named Achan has disregarded and violated the ban. The Israelites are routed and flee in utter defeat. Achan and his family were judged for his sin of rebellion. One may wonder if the judgment upon Achan and his family (capital punishment by stoning) is too harsh, but God hates rebellion against his will. And possibly more significant is the fact that the people *know* and remember that their parents spent forty years of wilderness wandering because of their corporate rebellion decades earlier. Rebellion had surfaced the first time their parents faced the challenge of conquering the land. They would not risk insurrection once again. The rebellious are annihilated! It was the only just solution.

These two battles in particular are highlighted specifically by Joshua to point out that the Lord is serious about two very crucial attitudes among his people: unbelief and rebellion. In short, I would suggest that these attitudes provide the most succinct definition of the biblical word known as "sin." What keeps us from walking with God? Lack of faith and disobedience. What prevents us from trusting and loving him? Lack of faith and disobedience. Unbelief hinders both our fellowship with God and our obedience in the Christian life. Rebellion keeps us from listening and responding to the will of God. Both attitudes keep us from honoring and glorifying God. God must continually search us and discipline us so that we will become people of both faith and wholehearted obedience.

After these tests in battle, and lessons in faith and obedience, the people of God return to Gilgal—their military headquarters—and assign the divisions of the land (Joshua chapters 13 and following). Attributing so much space to the description of land boundaries creates chapters that are tedious and laborious to read. But for the various tribes, knowing their assigned property lines is important. I am reminded of a story about a piece of property that my father purchased many years ago in Laurens County, South Carolina, not too far from Madden Station where he was born and grew up. He had a dream that someday he would leave Greenville, South Carolina, where he was a lawyer, and retire to return to Laurens County (my mother would not comply with those dreams.) As I recall, in the 1980s a man who had purchased a piece of property bordering my father's land came forward and declared that some of my father's property belonged to him. My father was convinced that the man was both dishonest and heavy handed, looking for a legal fight. The prospects of salvaging the land would involve an expensive and time consuming lawsuit. My father took the high road, deciding that the land was not worth fighting for in court, and eventually sold off his beloved piece of property. Property boundaries and markers are important, and although the chapters in Joshua describing them are lengthy, they will provide intertribal peace in time.

The last two chapters of the book of Joshua depict Joshua's parting words to his people, as he faces his impending death. In Joshua 23, he reminds them that the Lord God has fought for them and provided the inheritance of the land they are about to receive. He further warns them of the dangers ahead, particularly the peril of falling for the gods of the nations. Their God has kept his promises and they should keep his covenant. If you read Joshua 24:2–13, you will see Joshua recount the history of Israel—his own narration of their "progress of redemption." Joshua recounts the plan of God as it unfolds up until the present time of his parting exhortation. Based upon this gripping depiction of God's promise and their amazing deliverance as his special people, Joshua ends with a stirring speech. In light of all of the false gods that will face them in the Promised Land, he challenges the people of God to serve the Lord, the God of Israel. Joshua reminds them that God is the one who has faithfully and wonderfully delivered them!

JOSHUA - VICTORY

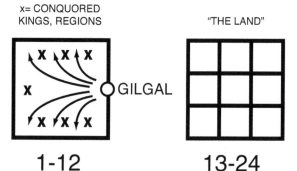

x= CONQUORED
KINGS, REGIONS

"THE LAND"

GILGAL

1-12
CONQUEST,
CONTROL

13-24
DIVISION,
ALLOTMENT

STEP SEVEN

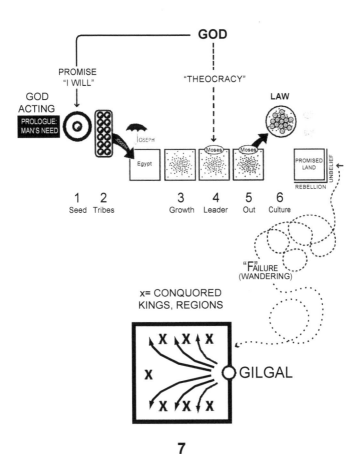

7
Victory
Jericho - deals with UNBELIEF
Ai - deals with REBELLION

Scene One

Step Eight

Judges

THE EVENTS COVERED IN the book of Joshua span approximately thirty years of time and include the overall theme of bright victory. In contrast, the various stories mentioned in the book of Judges span approximately three hundred and fifty years and include the overall theme of dark despair. The period of the judges is presented as a broad sweep of the history of Israel during very bleak days, after they finally dwell in the Promised Land. Chapter 2 provides a general summary of the entire book,

> ⁶ When Joshua dismissed the people, the people of Israel went each to his inheritance to take possession of the land. ⁷ And the people served the LORD all the days of Joshua, and all the days of the elders who outlived Joshua, who had seen all the great work that the LORD had done for Israel. ⁸ And Joshua the son of Nun, the servant of the LORD, died at the age of 110 years.

> ¹¹ And the people of Israel did what was evil in the sight of the LORD and served the Baals. ¹² And they abandoned the LORD, the God of their fathers, who had brought them out of the land of Egypt. They went after other gods, from among the gods of the peoples who were around them, and bowed down to them. And they provoked the LORD to anger. ¹³ They abandoned the LORD and served the Baals and the Ashtaroth. ¹⁴ So the anger of the LORD was kindled against Israel, and he gave them over to plunderers, who plundered them. And he sold them into the hand of

their surrounding enemies, so that they could no longer withstand their enemies.

¹⁶ Then the LORD raised up judges, who saved them out of the hand of those who plundered them. ¹⁷ Yet they did not listen to their judges, for they whored after other gods and bowed down to them. They soon turned aside from the way in which their fathers had walked, who had obeyed the commandments of the LORD, and they did not do so. ¹⁸ Whenever the LORD raised up judges for them, the LORD was with the judge, and he saved them from the hand of their enemies all the days of the judge. For the LORD was moved to pity by their groaning because of those who afflicted and oppressed them. ¹⁹ But whenever the judge died, they turned back and were more corrupt than their fathers, going after other gods, serving them and bowing down to them. They did not drop any of their practices or their stubborn ways. (Judg 2:6–8, 11–14, 16–19)

As seen by the description above, the stories of the judges follow a basic cycle: Sin (rebellion) → Servitude (retribution/discipline by the Lord) → Supplication (repentance) → Salvation (rest from their enemies). One can observe a few lessons about the Christian life by reading the stories of the various judges and watching how the Lord deals graciously with his people, especially when they fall into grave disobedience. He loves us enough to discipline us and to bring us to the joy of repentance and salvation.

The book is laid out in three distinct sections:

- Section One: Judges 1:1–2:5. The description of each tribe as they take the land; each tribe is its own political entity

- Section Two: Judges 2:6–16:31. A variety of stories explaining how God delivers his people through different judges at different times and places

- Section Three: Judges 17:1–21:25. Two stories are told that are indicative of the sad days during the times that the judges were raised up

In section one of the book of Judges, we read a constant refrain that is indicative of what happens when each tribe enters to take over its designated territory from the pagan residents living there. That refrain is, ". . . did not drive out the inhabitants . . ." (Judg 1:19, 21, 27, 28, 29, 30, 31, 32, 33). As each tribe moves into its own territory, it fails to obey the Lord's command to force out the respective tenants. In Judges 2:2–4, the Lord condemns his people for their failure to obey. He says,

"... and you shall make no covenant with the inhabitants of this land; you shall break down their altars.' But you have not obeyed my voice. What is this you have done? ³ So now I say, I will not drive them out before you, but they shall become thorns in your sides, and their gods shall be a snare to you." ⁴ As soon as the angel of the LORD spoke these words to all the people of Israel, the people lifted up their voices and wept.

The summary of section one is that the tribes have their land, but they do not fully conquer their enemies. They have no king or leader (like Joshua) to guide them to victory over God's enemies. This disheartening situation sets the stage for section two.

Without looking at the individual stories, section two can be summarized as God's raising up judges to deliver his people from enslavement to the local nations that remain in their respective areas of the Promised Land. Without a leader or king, life during the times of the judges could be characterized as "extremely unstable." We might wonder why there are various judges raised up. First, we need to remember that we are looking at a period of time that covers around three hundred and fifty years. Second, the judges are not placed or appointed over the entire nation, but are *regional* in nature, dealing with only a few tribes. Third, God raises up the judges both intermittently and without succession, based on the fact that they are needed only for a certain time and place. In the book of Judges, the second section (chapters 2:6–16:31) presents a series of stories about judges whom God uses to deliver his people.[1] We will not look at any of the stories about the individual judges. However, it is essential to note that, although these stories tell us many things about how God works on behalf of his people, these stories are provided for one basic purpose: *to create an awareness of need—the need for a king to rule over the nation.*

Section three (chapters 17–21) contains stories that would make the average (or maybe any) reader of the Bible shudder. Some wonder why stories such as these are included in Scripture. Yet these provocative accounts reveal what life, and even the people of God, become when God is absent

---

1. It is interesting to note that although Gideon is offered the role of king in Judges 8:22, in 8:23 he turns down the opportunity, while insightfully recognizing that the people need the Lord God to rule as king over them. Gideon understands that the biggest problem in the days of the judges is that the Lord is *not* king over his people. Additionally, in Judges 9:6, 50–57, Abimelech, son of Gideon, is a judge who becomes king through murderous and evil schemes, the opposite manner prescribed by the Lord as the way to ascend to the throne. His own people did not want to become subject to him; he dies in battle, ending a short and infamous reign.

from their midst; spiritual darkness prevails! In brief, the two accounts are simply anecdotal in nature and sadly reflect the state of Israel throughout the entire period of the times of the judges. The first story, found in chapters 17 and 18 of the book of Judges, portrays the rise of a man-made religion, carved images, and a false priesthood, all of which border on full-fledged superstition. In the midst of this darkness, God's light (his will and presence) have been lost. This one event displays the full-scale *idolatry* that is occurring during the days of the judges. The *worship* of the one, true living God of Israel has degenerated into gross corruption. This scene is a picture of how both God and the things of God are viewed. Idolatry always replaces the God of Israel.

The second story, found in chapters 19–21, appears much worse in its gloomy portrayal of moral degeneracy, but in some ways reflects the consequences of the graver sin of idolatry found in the previous two chapters. Where idolatry occurs, immorality is sure to follow. This story begins by describing a Levite (a priest) who is restored to his once unfaithful concubine. They then travel through a region where the tribe of Benjamin lives and are granted some gracious ancient near eastern hospitality. However, late in the evening, this male guest is approached by local men looking for homosexual experiences. To prevent such wickedness, staggering depravity is offered. The host offers his daughter and the traveler offers his concubine that these men may sexually abuse them, which they do all night to the concubine. Theirs is a crime of mob rape! The concubine dies from these ravages, the traveler takes her home, chops her body into pieces and sends her remains to all of the territories of Israel. Judges 19:30 tells us, "And all who saw it said, 'Such a thing has never happened or been seen from the day that the people of Israel came up out of the land of Egypt until this day; consider it, take counsel, and speak.'" War breaks out against the tribe of Benjamin; they are so soundly defeated that they are almost completely destroyed. This horrifying story displays the shocking nature of the sins that have overcome a people who have lost and forgotten their God: wickedness, homosexuality, mob rape, oppression, murder, and civil war and its consequences. In addition to the idolatry displayed in chapters 17–18, chapters 19–21 show us the gross *immorality* that has overtaken the nation of Israel during these days of judges. When God is absent relationships become corrupt, and sexual immorality, abuse, and hatred occur in plentiful quantities—always!

To summarize the book of Judges, there is a refrain that occurs four different times during the recounting of these two stories, one that explains the major problem of these days. That refrain appears in chapter 17 (verse 6), chapter 18 (verse 1), chapter 19 (verse 1), and chapter 21 (verse 25). This frequently repeated refrain is, "In those days there was no king in Israel. Everyone did what was right in his own eyes." The book of Judges closes with such a refrain because it summarizes the three hundred and fifty year period of spiritual darkness and ungodly living that characterizes the leaderless (or king-less) people of God. The people of God need a king with a heart for God. The purpose of a king who has God's heart is to prevent false worship and immoral behavior. Both destroy a culture and its people. What happens when there is no godly king ruling over God's people? Idolatry and immorality! In essence, idolatry and immorality are violations of the summary of the whole law: *love your God* with all your heart and with all your soul and with all your mind; and secondly: *love your neighbor* as yourself. Without a godly king to point the way, the will of God will always be violated or ignored.

Judges - No Leader/King

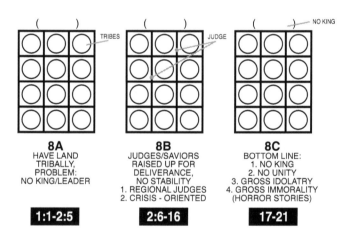

8A	8B	8C
HAVE LAND TRIBALLY, PROBLEM: NO KING/LEADER	JUDGES/SAVIORS RAISED UP FOR DELIVERANCE, NO STABILITY 1. REGIONAL JUDGES 2. CRISIS - ORIENTED	BOTTOM LINE: 1. NO KING 2. NO UNITY 3. GROSS IDOLATRY 4. GROSS IMMORALITY (HORROR STORIES)
1:1-2:5	**2:6-16**	**17-21**

Ruth

The book of Ruth seems to appear out of nowhere and yet it is properly set in Scripture next to the book of Judges with much relevance. Why is the book of Ruth recorded in God's story of redemption? Ruth 1:1 begins, "In the days when the judges ruled . . ." Those dark days of the judges, characterized by sexual immorality and idolatry, still retain a glimmer of light from the Lord. In the book of Judges, we see that, as bad as the people of God can become, there are still those who love God. Boaz is one of those shining lights. Boaz demonstrates his love for the Lord in the way that he treats his laborers, including the prime focus of the story, the Moabite woman known as Ruth (Ruth 2:8–12, 15–16).

We learn three powerful lessons from the short book of Ruth:

1. God has a remnant. There are still people, like Boaz, who love God and are not given over to the base sins of idolatry and immorality. Some still reflect the character of a follower of the God of Israel.

2. God includes the Gentiles in his plan of redemption. In the narrative of the book, Ruth is always called "the Moabite." She is designated as a person who is outside of the covenant people of God, but who is both brought into the covenant *and* shares in the blessings and benefits of being a member of God's covenant people.

3. Ruth is in the line *of the king*! Chapter 4 tells us, "Salmon fathered Boaz, Boaz fathered Obed, Obed fathered Jesse, and Jesse fathered David" (Ruth 4:21–22). It is quite amazing to see a non-Jew included in the *line* of the first true king of Israel. The formula that chapter 4 of Ruth presents is this: Ruth + Boaz → Obed → Jesse → King David. So significant is Ruth's part in the lineage of King David that the blessing she receives in chapter 4 of the book is powerful. Those elders and witnesses who observe Boaz's redemption of Ruth declare, "We are witnesses. May the LORD make the woman, who is coming into your house, like Rachel and Leah, who together built up the house of Israel" (Ruth 4:11). In this corporate declaration, Ruth "the Moabite" is exalted to the status of the women who helped fulfill the original seed promise to Abraham, Isaac, and Jacob! In addition to that declaration, these witnesses also make this wishful benediction, ". . . and may your house be like the house of Perez, whom Tamar bore to Judah, because of the offspring that the LORD will give you by this young woman" (Ruth 4:12). Indeed, the scepter shall not depart from the tribe of Judah, indicating the kingly line of Judah. And Ruth will be part of that kingly line![2]

2. A close study of the kingly line, traced from the original tribal leader, i.e., Judah,

The bottom line that must be noted in the book of Ruth is this: God is *still* working while everyone does what is right in his/her own eyes! And as we read about his grace, we bow our heads and thank him that he still works in our lives as well!

---

and running through to King David—and ultimately to Jesus—will reveal that God includes some of the least likely individuals in that royal line. Judah impregnates Tamar when she poses as a shrine prostitute in Genesis 38. Rahab, a former pagan harlot in Jericho, is included in the line of Boaz, as noted in Matthew 1:5. Ruth, a Gentile, becomes the wife of Boaz, and both are included in the line of King David, who, himself, is both an adulterer and murderer. In time, the ultimate, glorious and perfect king, Jesus, is born, without sin, having been conceived by the Holy Spirit, through the line of such fallen and seemingly out of place individuals.

STEP EIGHT

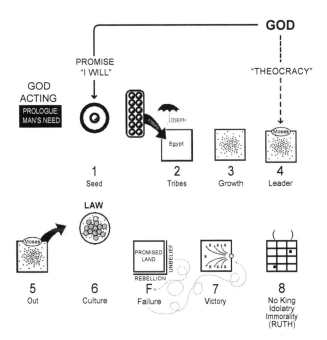

CYCLE OF THE JUDGES

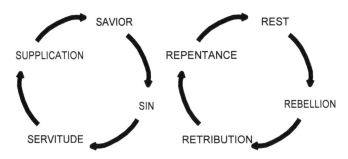

Scene One

Step Nine

Samuel: Period of Transition

1 Samuel Chapters 1–7

THE LIFE AND MINISTRY of Samuel occurs during the times of the judges and begins in the most unexpected and yet also expected circumstances. Samuel's father is a man named Elkanah. Elkanah has two wives—his polygamy probably being a sign that he is living in the dark period of the times of the judges! One wife is Hannah, whom he dearly loves, and the other is named Penninah. Penninah has children, but as expected (from previous Old Testament narratives), Hannah is barren (1 Sam 1:2, 5). The sovereign Lord has closed Hannah's womb! Penninah gloats over Hannah regarding her children and Hannah's inability to conceive, but Hannah, in her grief, maintains hope in the Lord. We have previously seen and learned that the Lord can do whatever he wills with barren women. When Elkanah and Hannah take a visit to the temple, the text tells us,

> Now Eli the priest was sitting on the seat beside the doorpost of the temple of the LORD. [10] She was deeply distressed and prayed to the LORD and wept bitterly. [11] And she vowed a vow and said, "O LORD of hosts, if you will indeed look on the affliction of your servant and remember me and not forget your servant, but will give to your servant a son, then I will give him to the LORD all the days of his life, and no razor shall touch his head." (1 Sam 1:9b–11)

As we read these lines, we conclude that Hannah not only wants a child, but wants a son. And why a son? She has a deeper motive for wanting to give birth to a child. She reasons with the Lord—if you give me a boy, I will give him to you. With stunning insight, Hannah realizes, living in the times of the judges, that Israel needs a man. Israel needs a leader: a king—everyone is doing what is right in their own eyes. So, if granted a son, she will give him to God. In 1 Samuel 1:11, Hannah declares that a razor shall not touch his head, i.e., he shall be a Nazarite, or one totally dedicated to the Lord. As she prays a deeply heartfelt prayer, Hannah's lips move, but her voice is not heard. Eli, the priest who is watching her pray, rebukes her for being drunk in the temple. Of course, Hannah is not drunk. She is deeply affected by her passion and prayers for a son. But sadly, this picture speaks forcefully about the days of the judges. Apparently, people often came to the temple while drunk! It is difficult to imagine people today coming to church to worship in a drunken state, but this is the days of the judges!

In 1 Samuel 1:24, we read that Samuel is weaned and dedicated to the Lord, most probably at age three (it was not out of the ordinary in those days for a child to breastfeed through three years of age.) Hannah then lends (or gives) Samuel to the Lord and Samuel worships the Lord there. Hannah's sacrifice would be like a modern day parent giving up their child to a mission school on the mission field, and leaving him/her behind. In light of this great sacrifice, Hannah's prayer in 1 Samuel 2:1–10 is quite amazing (take a moment to read it)!

Following Hannah's dedication of Samuel, we return to the realities of spiritual life in Israel, taking a closer look at the sons of Eli, the priest. "Now the sons of Eli were worthless men. They did not know the LORD" (1 Sam 2:12). We are told in 1 Samuel 2:17 that Eli's sons are treating the offerings brought to the temple with contempt. They see the offerings only as food items for themselves and not as sacred offerings given unto the Lord. They do not "fear" the Lord by properly carrying out the sacrificial instructions (Lev 7:30–34). Their actions are *idolatrous* acts of worship. Secondly, the text tells us that Eli's sons sleep with the women who serve at the entrance of the tent of meeting. Upon hearing this, Eli tries to rebuke his sons, but to no avail. They are guilty of *sexual immorality*. Idolatry and immorality—these two grave sins are indicative of the days of the judges (remember Judg 17–21). Not only are these two sins pervasive in the present Israelite culture, they are part of the priestly culture and line! What dark days exist in Israel. Amazingly, this is the context in which Samuel will be raised! How Israel needs a man of God to lead them!

In Samuel chapter 3, we see Samuel's call from God. Verse 1 tells us, "Now the boy Samuel was ministering to the LORD in the presence of Eli. And the word of the LORD was rare in those days; there was no frequent vision." In the past, the Lord had spoken clearly to Moses and also revealed himself directly with Joshua, but for three hundred and fifty years, he has only sporadically intervened, and very rarely was there one who could be called a prophet. Eli, old and with dim vision, goes to bed while Samuel lies down in the temple beside the ark. The Lord calls his name three times, though Samuel thinks it is Eli who is calling. Verse 7 gives the reader insight into the situation: "Now Samuel did not yet know the LORD, and the word of the LORD had not yet been revealed to him." What do these words mean? Samuel has ministered before the Lord (1 Sam 2:18), and previously has worshipped the Lord (1 Sam 1:28). However, the inference is that Samuel is not yet a recipient of direct revelation from God, i.e., a prophet.

The voice of God is calling to Samuel for a holy purpose. Verses 10–14 tell us what happens next,

> And the LORD came and stood, calling as at other times, "Samuel! Samuel!" And Samuel said, "Speak, for your servant hears." [11] Then the LORD said to Samuel, "Behold, I am about to do a thing in Israel at which the two ears of everyone who hears it will tingle. [12] On that day I will fulfill against Eli all that I have spoken concerning his house, from beginning to end. [13] And I declare to him that I am about to punish his house forever, for the iniquity that he knew, because his sons were blaspheming God, and he did not restrain them. [14] Therefore I swear to the house of Eli that the iniquity of Eli's house shall not be atoned for by sacrifice or offering forever." (1 Sam 3:10–14)

The Lord is calling Samuel *to hear* from him (which Samuel gladly does) and *to speak* on his behalf, even if the news is bad (such as judgment on Eli's house). Samuel is to become a prophet (the spokesman) of God. We might call him *the* prophet of God for the coming era, a period of transition. Samuel is the first "full-time" or professional prophet of Israel. Being a prophet is his identity and vocation. Israel has a priestly line in place (Lev chapters 8–10). Moses had served in a combination role as a prophet and a king, but could not maintain those roles as Israel grew too large to be managed by one man. Israel obviously needs a "full time" king—tragically, every person throughout the nation is doing what is right in his own eyes. God is in the process of preparing an administration designed to allow for the functioning of a large nation. Israel is soon to see the development of all three offices that shall be a part of their existence as a nation: prophet, priest, and king.

Samuel will fulfill the role of prophet to Israel, and the timing of his calling is providential. The summary of his calling to, and growth in, his prophetic ministry is written in 1 Samuel 3:19–21,

> And Samuel grew, and the LORD was with him and let none of his words fall to the ground. [20] And all Israel from Dan to Beersheba knew that Samuel was established as a prophet of the LORD. [21] And the LORD appeared again at Shiloh, for the LORD revealed himself to Samuel at Shiloh by the word of the LORD.

The important phrase in this passage involves the words "all Israel." The Lord speaks, verifies Samuel's words, and *all* Israel acknowledges him as a prophet of the Lord. At a time when there was no king in Israel and everyone was doing what was right in his/her own eyes, God places a man who will not only speak for him, but who will lead the people in the will of the Lord. Samuel's prophetic role brings *unity* to a nation that has suffered from its absence for hundreds of years.

The unity of Israel under the prophet Samuel is the emphasis of the first three chapters of the book of 1 Samuel. Chapters 4–7 demonstrate the nature of the unity. In chapter 4, verse 1, after we are reminded of the unity of Israel under Samuel, we read that the Israelites (or "all Israel") initiate a battle with their enemies, the Philistines. Though the Israelite troops appear to have military unity, they lose the battle. Upon their defeat, they turn to the ark of the covenant for help. What they express is significant, "Why has the LORD defeated us today before the Philistines? Let us bring the ark of the covenant of the LORD here from Shiloh, that it may come among us and save us from the power of our enemies" (1 Sam 4:3). Essentially, they treat the ark either as a god in and of itself, or as a superstitious good luck charm that can bring about salvation and deliverance. Their attitude is appalling, idolatrous, and leads to another defeat. They also lose the ark to the Philistines, much to the dismay (and demise) of any Philistine community that possesses it. God is against all those that keep the ark (1 Sam 5:9, 11–12). In chapter 6, the ark is returned to Israel and in chapter 7, the climax of the story is unveiled.

From the day that the ark was lodged at Kiriath-jearim, a long time passed, some twenty years, and all the house of Israel lamented after the LORD. [3] And Samuel said to all the house of Israel, "If you are returning to the LORD with all your heart, then put away the foreign gods and the Ashtaroth from among you and direct your heart to the LORD and serve him only, and he will deliver you out of the hand of the Philistines." [4] So the people of Israel put away the Baals and the Ashtaroth, and they served the LORD only. [5] Then Samuel said, "Gather all Israel at Mizpah, and I will pray to the LORD for you." (1 Sam 7:2–5)

Once again, we are told that *all* Israel responds to their need of the Lord. *All* seek after the Lord (verse 2), Samuel speaks to *all* Israel (verse 3) and gathers *all* Israel at Mizpah (verse 5). In response, they sincerely turn to the Lord, put away their false gods and idols, and confess their sins together. Today, we would call this a national revival!

The text also provides a second summary statement about Samuel. We are twice told that Samuel "judged" Israel (verses 6 and 15). The bottom line to step nine is that Samuel, *the prophet*, both *unites* the people and points them to the Lord alone for deliverance. He also *judges* them all for the rest of his life! When he passes away, his sons become judges (1 Sam 8:1). Samuel, as the first prophet (full-time), as well as the last judge, functions as a "mini-king" for the people of Israel. He leads them to the Lord, speaks his word with authority, and judges (or rules) over them. Israel, after centuries of faithlessness, idolatry, and other sins that have made the presence of the judges unavoidable, is finally united under the Lord, the God of Israel, because of Samuel's call. Is this progress? Are we ready for a king? Read on!

STEP NINE

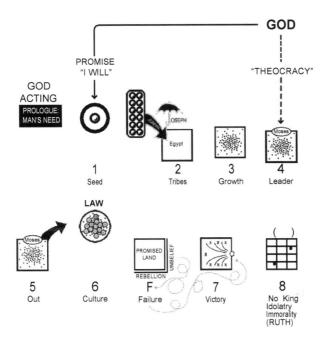

1	2	3	4
Seed	Tribes	Growth	Leader

5	6	F	7	8
Out	Culture	Failure	Victory	No King
				Idolatry
				Immorality
				(RUTH)

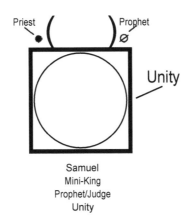

Samuel
Mini-King
Prophet/Judge
Unity

Scene One

Step Ten

Saul: Monarchy

1 Samuel Chapters 8–15

Saul Accepted: 1 Samuel Chapters 8–12

As WE WATCH THE progress that the Lord has brought to pass thus far, we are able to conclude that Israel is ready for a king. We have a multitude of people, a tribal framework, laws and culture, occupied land, a kingly lineage, leaders (judges, prophets, and priests), a mini-king in Samuel, and the unity necessary for the nation to listen corporately to their ultimate king, the Lord. However, as we observe Samuel's sons, men who were appointed as judges to assume his position, we recognize a reality that commonly occurs in Scripture: often the offspring of spiritual leaders do not follow the ways of their parents. In regard to Samuel's sons, 1 Samuel 8:3 tells us, "Yet his sons did not walk in his ways but turned aside after gain. They took bribes and perverted justice." This failure in leadership transferral further indicates a need for a king, and a godly one at that. As Samuel ages and his sons continue in their evil ways, the people recognize that there is no future for them with Samuel's sons. So they turn to Samuel and say, "Behold, you are old and your sons do not walk in your ways. Now appoint for us a king to judge us like all the nations" (1 Sam 8:5). Samuel is displeased because he thinks the request is a reflection upon himself. But the Lord tells Samuel that they have not rejected Samuel; rather, they have rejected the Lord.

As we read later in the text, there are a number of times that the people's request is misguided:

- The people of Israel want to be like the other nations, i.e., a pure, human monarchy, ruled by an earthly king. The Lord wants a theocracy, i.e., God ruling over his people through a man of his choosing and one who has a heart for him (1 Sam 8:18–22).
- They have rejected God as their king (1 Sam 10:17–19).
- They appear jealous of the surrounding nations that are ruled by their own kings. Their interest is in becoming a "secular" nation, not a nation of the Lord (1 Sam 12:12).

In 1 Samuel 12:17–18, Samuel tells the people that he will call upon the Lord to send thunder and rain to show them that their request for a king is a request stemming from their wickedness. They have lost all apparent spiritual focus on the Lord. What is wrong with their request for a king?

- They ask for the wrong *thing*: a monarchy (1 Sam 8:4–5).
- They ask with the wrong *motive*: to be like the other nations (1 Sam 8:5).
- They ask the wrong *person*: they turn to Samuel to make their request instead of calling out to the Lord (1 Sam 8:4–5).

In 1 Samuel 9, we read the story of Saul's choosing by God and the beginning of his ascension to the throne of Israel. By appearances, Saul strikes us as a potential leader. He comes from an esteemed family, is tall, handsome, and stands above the people. God chooses him as the people's leader, declaring that he will use Saul to lead the nation over their enemies, the Philistines (1 Sam 9:15–16). Samuel then anoints Saul in a private anointing of sorts (1 Sam 10:1). The Spirit of the Lord comes upon him (1 Sam 10:6) and the Lord gives Saul a new heart (1 Sam 10:9–11). The public acknowledgement of Saul as king occurs in the ensuing verses. Samuel sorts through the various tribes by lot and Benjamin is selected. Eventually, Saul is determined, by lot, out of the sons of Benjamin to be the king. This process is something like a public election, though ultimately Saul is chosen by God. When Saul is chosen and needs to be confirmed, he cannot be found—he is hiding behind the baggage, seemingly displaying humility, as well as reluctance to assume this daunting role.

In 1 Samuel 11, as would be expected, Saul's leadership is immediately challenged. The Ammonites besiege the people of Jabesh-Gilead, oppressing them by threatening to gouge out their right eyes (1 Sam 11:1–4). Saul is incensed at hearing such evil, an affront to God's people. He rallies the people of Israel to fight against the Ammonites. The dread of the Lord (not Saul) falls upon the people, and under Saul's leadership they prevail (1 Sam 11:6–7, 11). We see God's victory through his chosen agent! Samuel appeals to the people to congregate at Gilgal and there Saul is "inaugurated" as King Saul of Israel; this is a day of rejoicing! (1 Sam 11:14–15). Saul's victories are summarized in 1 Samuel 14:47–48,

> When Saul had taken the kingship over Israel, he fought against all his enemies on every side, against Moab, against the Ammonites, against Edom, against the kings of Zobah, and against the Philistines. Wherever he turned he routed them. [48] And he did valiantly and struck the Amalekites and delivered Israel out of the hands of those who plundered them.

The Lord has used Saul to conquer Israel's enemies on every side—a working theocracy is the result of these great national battles! On the surface, it appears that we have the right king at the right time. It appears that we have finally reached the first goal of Abraham's promise—a great nation formed and led by both the Lord and his chosen man. It appears that we have a theocracy. I wonder if, when hearing this story, the Maasai tribe would be curious about this picture. Does it look right or not?

Saul Rejected: 1 Samuel 13–15

Saul has been chosen, anointed, and blessed by God. However, the battles with the surrounding nations continue and Saul faces a very difficult foe once more, the dreaded Philistines. In 1 Samuel 13:5 we read that the belligerent Philistines arise once again and are so forceful that the Israelite soldiers tremble and flee in all directions. Saul is deeply worried. Citing the text is most helpful in recounting what happens,

> He waited seven days, the time appointed by Samuel. But Samuel did not come to Gilgal, and the people were scattering from him. [9] So Saul said, "Bring the burnt offering here to me, and the peace offerings." And he offered the burnt offering. [10] As soon as he had finished offering the burnt offering, behold, Samuel came. And Saul went out to meet him and greet him. [11] Samuel said, "What

have you done?" And Saul said, "When I saw that the people were scattering from me, and that you did not come within the days appointed, and that the Philistines had mustered at Michmash, [12] I said, 'Now the Philistines will come down against me at Gilgal, and I have not sought the favor of the LORD.' So I forced myself, and offered the burnt offering." [13] And Samuel said to Saul, "You have done foolishly. You have not kept the command of the LORD your God, with which he commanded you. For then the LORD would have established your kingdom over Israel forever. [14] But now your kingdom shall not continue. The LORD has sought out a man after his own heart, and the LORD has commanded him to be prince over his people, because you have not kept what the LORD commanded you." (1 Sam 13:8–14)

Saul, as king, takes upon himself the priestly role, offering a burnt offering, hoping to gain favor from the Lord in the thick of battle. He has failed miserably as a spiritual leader for God's people. Samuel tells Saul that he could have had an established line (of sons) on the throne of Israel forever—a theocracy—but his foolish act has brought upon him God's rejection. This is *rejection number one*: Saul's descendants will not retain their place as those who will inherit the kingdom. His throne will not be perpetuated.

In 1 Samuel 15, we read another significantly sad account in the life of King Saul. The Lord sends him to fight the Amalekites, and to destroy them and everything they own. It is a simple and comprehensive command. Saul does defeat the Amalekites, but the text speaks of his disobedience and failure,

> And he took Agag the king of the Amalekites alive and devoted to destruction all the people with the edge of the sword. [9] But Saul and the people spared Agag and the best of the sheep and of the oxen and of the fattened calves and the lambs, and all that was good, and would not utterly destroy them. All that was despised and worthless they devoted to destruction. (1 Sam 15:8–9)

Saul is disobedient to God's command, destroying the bad and keeping the good as a spoil of battle, rather than destroying everything. He is guilty of rebellion, a sin that God despises. In an almost humorous scene, Samuel comes to Saul and upon his arrival asks this question, "What then is this bleating of the sheep in my ears and the lowing of the oxen that I hear?" (1 Sam 15:14). Saul's disobedience cannot only be seen but heard! His disobedience is quite public and as a leader of God's people, such rebellion must be judged. Saul deceives himself, justifying his actions by reasoning that he could sacrifice, unto the Lord, all of the healthy animals he has retained. Samuel immediately teaches Saul the way of godliness when he declares,

> "Has the LORD as great delight in burnt offerings and sacrifices, as in obeying the voice of the LORD? Behold, *to obey is better than sacrifice,* and to listen than the fat of rams. [23] For rebellion is as the sin of divination, and presumption is as iniquity and idolatry. Because you have rejected the word of the LORD, he has also rejected you from being king." (1 Sam 15:22–23, italics mine for emphasis)

Not only are Saul's descendants rejected from the kingdom line, (rejection number one) but Saul himself is rejected as king. This is *rejection number two.* He will be replaced by a king who has a heart for God. And although Saul confesses his sins against God, it is too late. His reign will be over in due time.

Graham Scroggie provides two insightful quotes that summarize Saul's biography and serve as epithets. "Saul is the most pathetic, tragic, and mysterious of Bible personalities"[1]; and, "This man had no deep-seated religious principle, no fear of God that influenced his life. His day began in bright sunshine, by noon thick clouds began to gather, and night overtook him in tragedy."[2] We close section ten with our perpetual question, "Is there any progress in this step?" This question is difficult to answer. The best we can say is that in the midst of failure, God is raising up a king, a man with a heart for God! That brings us to step eleven.

---

1. Scroggie, *Unfolding Drama,* 242.
2. Ibid., 242.

STEP TEN

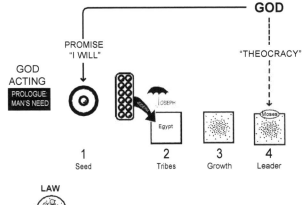

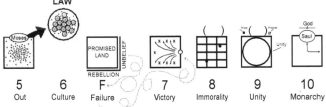

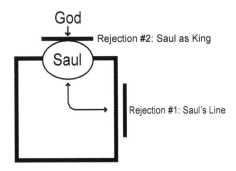

Theocracy Becomes Monarchy

Scene One

Step Eleven

Theocracy

David/Solomon

1 Samuel 16–2 Samuel

DAVID

THIS SECTION IS SO important that it is covered in two different historical records, 1 and 2 Samuel and 1 and 2 Chronicles. We have finally reached the stage where an authentic theocracy is truly ready to be established. In 1 Samuel 16, we read that the Lord has chosen Saul's replacement. Interestingly, God doesn't tell Samuel who the man might be. Among the sons of Jesse, Samuel has to discern which son will be God's choice. God is teaching Samuel (and all of us) a great lesson about leadership in his kingdom. After sorting through the first son, Eliab, and wondering if he would be Israel's next leader, based upon his outward appearance alone, the Lord states, "Do not look on his appearance or on the height of his stature, because I have rejected him. For the LORD sees not as man sees: man looks on the outward appearance, but the LORD looks on the heart" (1 Sam 16:7). Samuel proceeds to contemplate multiple sons and cannot find the right one. There is one remaining, however, the youngest, a son keeping sheep, named David. The text tells us that when this son arrives, he is ruddy (reddish or outdoorish), has beautiful eyes, and is handsome. The Lord tells

Samuel to anoint him (a private anointing) and when he does, the Spirit of God rushes upon David. He is a man with a heart for God!

However, David does not ascend immediately to the throne; it will be ten to fifteen years before he will replace Saul as king. We will watch David ascend to the throne eventually, but in the meantime, the Lord will take him through his own royal training program. 1 Samuel 17 is a picture of David's training and potential for leadership. As Israel's troops cower in the presence of Goliath the Philistine enemy, David arrives and asks the bold, and frankly amazing, question, "For who is this uncircumcised Philistine, that he should defy the armies of the living God?" (1 Sam 17:26). Before Saul, he recounts some of his past experiences in dealing with danger in the strength of the Lord,

> And Saul said to David, "You are not able to go against this Phi-
> listine to fight with him, for you are but a youth, and he has been
> a man of war from his youth." 34 But David said to Saul, "Your
> servant used to keep sheep for his father. And when there came
> a lion, or a bear, and took a lamb from the flock, 35 I went after
> him and struck him and delivered it out of his mouth. And if he
> arose against me, I caught him by his beard and struck him and
> killed him. 36 Your servant has struck down both lions and bears,
> and this uncircumcised Philistine shall be like one of them, for he
> has defied the armies of the living God." 37 And David said, "The
> LORD who delivered me from the paw of the lion and from the
> paw of the bear will deliver me from the hand of this Philistine."
> (1 Sam 17:33–37)

David has learned to trust God. But can he lead? His first "theocratic" test of leadership is found in this confrontation with the symbol of the enemies of God, the giant named Goliath. He declares the following to this Philistine, "You come to me with a sword and with a spear and with a javelin, but I come to you in the name of the LORD of hosts, the God of the armies of Israel, whom you have defied" (1 Sam 17:45). Young David doesn't rely upon the weapons of battle, but stands in opposition to God's enemies relying solely upon the strength and help of the Lord. The narrative continues, "So David prevailed over the Philistine with a sling and with a stone, and struck the Philistine and killed him. There was no sword in the hand of David" (1 Sam 17:50). David conquers the Lord's enemies fully dependent upon the help of the Lord. This is the lesson of David and Goliath. God is the helper of his people, and we must rely upon and have faith in him in order to live the Christian life. David believes in the lesson learned at Jericho, "God will do it!" Faith is the key! Interestingly, in every subsequent battle, David uses the sword to fight. But in this first test, he prevails by faith and a sling. His first theocratic test: David versus Goliath. A+ is his score!

1 Samuel 18–23 is a record of Saul's jealousy and persecution of David, who has become Saul's royal competition. These chapters are a picture of Saul's attempt to rule his circumstances by his own strength (since he no longer seeks the Lord), and of David learning to depend wholly on God for day-to-day survival. In 1 Samuel 24, we read about David's second "theocratic" test. Saul enters a dark cave in order to relieve himself, while being fully unaware that David and some of his men are hiding in the recesses of the cave. The text tells us what happens next:

> And the men of David said to him, "Here is the day of which the Lord said to you, 'Behold, I will give your enemy into your hand, and you shall do to him as it shall seem good to you.'" Then David arose and stealthily cut off a corner of Saul's robe. 5 And afterward David's heart struck him, because he had cut off a corner of Saul's robe. 6 He said to his men, "The Lord forbid that I should do this thing to my lord, the Lord's anointed, to put out my hand against him, seeing he is the Lord's anointed." 7 So David persuaded his men with these words and did not permit them to attack Saul. And Saul rose up and left the cave and went on his way. (1 Sam 24:4–7)

David's men use the phrase "your enemy." Yet, they are not talking about the Philistines; rather, they are addressing Saul, the king of Israel. We are told that in the midst of the temptation to do harm to Saul, David's heart bothers him. He is convicted of his own sin. He repents and confesses that the Lord is his sovereign. He cannot harm the one who is "the Lord's anointed." David is clearly a man after God's own heart. His second theocratic test: David versus his persecutor, the king of Israel. His score: A++!

David has learned how to trust God with regard to his enemies. The Philistines are his enemy "on the outside" and Saul is his enemy "on the inside" (or within the camp). If only today Christ followers could trust God to take care of their enemies, whether outside the church or in, we would be very different people! In 1 Samuel 26, we see David spare Saul's life a second time. We are viewing the spiritual maturity of a man with a heart after the Lord. David understands that it is not his role to climb the ladder of success, while stepping over, or on, others who might be in his way. Although the opportunity is before him, and others tell him that the Lord has created an open door for him to assert himself and become king, we see that David is not going to put himself on the top of the kingdom. And although he has been anointed to become the next king of Israel, he leaves the process to make that happen completely in the Lord's hands.

In 2 Samuel 1, we are given a second account of Saul's (and his sons') death (the first account occurs in 1 Samuel 31:1-7). We could easily conclude that David is ready and thus should naturally assume the kingship of Israel. Yet, that doesn't happen; David hesitates to ascend to the throne of the kingdom. This scenario reminds me of an anecdote I heard while I was a senior student in seminary. A representative from my denomination spoke at one of our chapel services and told us that he was in charge of starting churches throughout the United States for our new and young denomination. He said that his church planting committee had recently advertised two different church planting opportunities, both being very different from the other. He explained that one new church need was located in the state of New Jersey, while the other new church was needed in the state of Hawaii. He said that only two prospective pastors had applied for the church start up in New Jersey, while over two hundred applicants clearly believed that "it was God's will for their lives that they start a church plant planned for Hawaii!" Of course! Saul is now gone. It would seem natural for David that he should ascend to the vacant throne. But the text tells us that David, rather than making this most obvious move, appeals to the Lord, "Shall I go up into any of the cities of Judah?" (2 Sam 2:1). This is a question indicating that David wonders if he should "go public" as the next king. The Lord tells him to go. Here is a man who does not presume to know the Lord's will. He seeks the avenue of prayer prior to making a decision, as obvious as that decision might be! In verse 4, we read, "And the men of Judah came, and there they anointed David king over the house of Judah."

David ascends to the royal throne. However, in 2 Samuel chapter 3, we discover once again that nothing comes easy, even when the will of the Lord is clear. Saul's family fights David's family for the throne. David, of course, prevails. In 2 Samuel chapter 5 we read,

> Then *all the tribes of Israel* came to David at Hebron and said, "Behold, we are your bone and flesh. ² In times past, when Saul was king over us, it was you who led out and brought in Israel. And the LORD said to you, 'You shall be shepherd of my people Israel, and you shall be prince over Israel.'" ³ So all the elders of Israel came to the king at Hebron, and King David made a covenant with them at Hebron before the LORD, and they anointed David king over Israel (1–30). (italics mine, for emphasis)

A landmark event has finally occurred. David is now king over *all* of Israel! For the first time ever, the earth has a theocratic nation!! Abraham would be amazed. The Maasai tribal people would be celebrating. So much progress has transpired and God's nation on earth has finally materialized!

The function of a king is to rule. Ruling involves both maintaining righteousness in the nation, and conquering the kingdom's enemies (i.e., maintaining peace). Immediately, as might be expected, David's royal position is challenged. Israel's chronic nemesis, the Philistines, confront David in order to defy him. David's newly acknowledged leadership is being tested directly. Yet, we watch David's posture once again—he bows before the Lord. "Shall I go up against the Philistines? Will you give them into my hand?" (2 Sam 5:19). Fighting the Philistines is an obvious task and role for the king of Israel. But, this king is a theocratic leader. He knows that God's will must prevail over his own will in order for his kingdom to prevail over the enemies of God's kingdom. The Lord tells David, "Go up, for I will certainly give the Philistines into your hand" (2 Sam 5:19). Israel, under David, conquers the Philistines. A few verses later (an indefinite amount of time has passed), we are told that the Philistines arise against David once more. Although having been victorious previously over these persistent pagans, David presumes nothing. Once again, he inquires of the Lord. God tells him not to attack them in the same manner, but to use a different strategy: "Trick 'em!" The concluding verse of the chapter summarizes David's heart for God, a heart of submission and obedience, "And David did as the LORD commanded him, and struck down the Philistines from Geba to Gezer" (2 Sam 5:25).

In 2 Samuel chapter 8, we read the historian's summary of David's leadership as king over Israel. Verse 11 says, "These also King David dedicated to the LORD, together with the silver and gold that he dedicated from *all the nations he subdued . . .*" (italics mine, for emphasis). David conquers his enemies and experiences victories for his people. Verse 15 states, "So David reigned over all Israel. And David administered justice and equity to all his people." As a king, David provides justice to his people. The functions of government are to keep its people safe from their enemies, to bring them peace, and to assure its people that justice will reign. Providing victory for and maintaining righteousness in the nation are dual attributes of royalty. David's kingdom reflects the "victory" theme found in the book of Joshua and provides the "righteousness and justice" missing in the book of Judges. His reign brings very positive contributions to the theocracy of God!

We must note that in 2 Samuel, chapter 7, David expresses a desire to build the Lord a house (or temple). Nathan, the prophet, encourages him to do so, but then the Lord speaks to Nathan. God tells Nathan to explain to David that because he is a man of war and bloodshed, God will raise up an offspring from David to build a house for his name. The Lord tells Nathan,

> Moreover, the LORD declares to you that the LORD will make you a house. [12] When your days are fulfilled and you lie down with your fathers, I will raise up your offspring after you, who shall come from your body, and I will establish his kingdom. [13] He shall build a house for my name, and I will establish the throne of his kingdom forever. (2 Sam 7:11–13)

And also, "And your house and your kingdom shall be made sure forever before me. Your throne shall be established forever" (2 Sam 7:16). This is the great covenant with David. God promises that David's kingdom will never cease and that it will always have a king on the throne. The great Davidic covenant is the second great covenant of God with his people. God made the Abrahamic covenant containing a two-fold promise: a nation will come from his seed, and ultimately that seed shall bring a blessing to all of the world! David's reign as king over Israel is the capstone of the first promise and is also a picture of a kingdom whose king will always reign, and whose kingdom (the people, community, or seed of God) will always be! This is a picture of Christ and his church!

As the narrative about David's ascent to the throne of Israel continues, we are brought to the conclusion that in order to serve the Lord, God does not require us to be perfect. As his followers we should strive for the holiness without which no one will see the Lord. But in David's life, as described by the scriptures, we are confronted with a horrific account of sexual sin (adultery), murder, cover up, and more. David's lust and passion for Bathsheba demonstrates that he isn't perfect. Nevertheless, his godly sorrow and repentance, as expressed particularly in the penitential psalms (6, 32, 38, 51), display that David has a perfect heart. A perfect heart is one that is submissive to God, as well as contrite over sin, while trusting fully in the Lord's forgiveness and help in time of trial.

SOLOMON

If King David contributes justice, righteousness, and victory to the nation (or kingdom) that God has built, King Solomon contributes so much more. We read of Solomon's reign in 1 Kings, chapters 1–10 (his birth is mentioned in 2 Samuel 12:24). In 1 Kings chapter 1, we read that David has become very old and his death is impending. One of his sons, Adonijah, "exalts himself," declaring that he will be the next king of Israel. He is obviously not "a man after God's own heart." And once again, we see that nothing comes easy in God's kingdom. Adonijah's revolt is squashed and Solomon ascends to the throne that is properly his. In 1 Kings 2:12, we read, "So Solomon sat on the throne of David his father, and his kingdom was firmly established." Under Solomon's reign, some very significant benefits attend the kingdom of Israel.

1. Instead of the posture of war that David's reign typifies, Solomon's kingdom is one epitomized by *peace*. "For he had dominion over all the region west of the Euphrates from Tiphsah to Gaza, over all the kings west of the Euphrates. And he had peace on all sides around him" (1 Kgs 4:24). The nation of Israel experiences *rest* from her foes, much like the rest granted when the Lord provided salvation through the saviors he sends during the period of the judges (See also 1 Kgs 4:21).

2. Solomon's kingdom is one of *wisdom*, in which the wisdom that is granted to him is derived from God. "And God gave Solomon wisdom and understanding beyond measure, and breadth of mind like the sand on the seashore, [30] so that Solomon's wisdom surpassed the wisdom of all the people of the east and all the wisdom of Egypt" (1 Kgs 4:29–30). Solomon's wisdom is theocratic wisdom, wisdom for ruling God's people. Of course, the wisdom of Solomon and how he received it is one of the more famous stories of the Bible,

> At Gibeon the LORD appeared to Solomon in a dream by night, and God said, "Ask what I shall give you." [6] And Solomon said, "You have shown great and steadfast love to your servant David my father, because he walked before you in faithfulness, in righteousness, and in uprightness of heart toward you. And you have kept for him this great and steadfast love and have given him a son to sit on his throne this day. [7] And now, O LORD my God, you have made your servant king in place of David my father, although I am but a little child. I do not know how to go out or come in. [8] And your servant is in the midst of your people whom you have chosen, a great people, too many to be numbered or counted for multitude. [9] Give your servant

therefore an understanding mind to govern your people, that I may discern between good and evil, for who is able to govern this your great people?" [10] It pleased the Lord that Solomon had asked this. [11] And God said to him, "Because you have asked this, and have not asked for yourself long life or riches or the life of your enemies, but have asked for yourself understanding to discern what is right, [12] behold, I now do according to your word. Behold, I give you a wise and discerning mind, so that none like you has been before you and none like you shall arise after you." (1 Kgs 3:5–12)

3. Solomon's wisdom provides a continuation of the *justice* that David's kingdom displayed. "And all Israel heard of the judgment that the king had rendered, and they stood in awe of the king, because they perceived that the wisdom of God was in him to do justice" (1 Kgs 3:28).

4. There is *victory and dominion* over Israel's surrounding enemies. "Solomon ruled over all the kingdoms from the Euphrates to the land of the Philistines and to the border of Egypt. They brought tribute and served Solomon all the days of his life" (1 Kgs 4:21).

5. There is a deep sense of *safety* given to the people because of Solomon's dominion. "And Judah and Israel lived in safety, from Dan even to Beersheba, every man under his vine and under his fig tree, all the days of Solomon" (1 Kgs 4:25).

6. The peace granted by Solomon's treaties with the surrounding enemy nations creates a people filled with joy and *happiness*. "Judah and Israel were as many as the sand by the sea. They ate and drank and were happy" (1 Kgs 4:20).

7. There is *wealth* beyond measure,

> And when the queen of Sheba had seen all the wisdom of Solomon, the house that he had built, [5] the food of his table, the seating of his officials, and the attendance of his servants, their clothing, his cupbearers, and his burnt offerings that he offered at the house of the LORD, there was no more breath in her.[6] And she said to the king, "The report was true that I heard in my own land of your words and of your wisdom, [7] but I did not believe the reports until I came and my own eyes had seen it. And behold, the half was not told me. Your wisdom and prosperity surpass the report that I heard." (1 Kgs 10:4–7)

8. As observed in the Queen of Sheba's visit, *the world is coming* to see the glory of the king!

9. Solomon spends seven years building the *temple* that David wanted to build.

10. Once the temple is built, Solomon brings the ark of the covenant—symbolizing the presence of the Lord—into the temple and *the glory of the Lord* falls down upon the temple. "And when the priests came out of the Holy Place, a cloud filled the house of the LORD, [11] so that the priests could not stand to minister because of the cloud, for the glory of the LORD filled the house of the LORD" (1 Kgs 8:10–11). The falling of God's glory is almost beyond imagination and I don't think that we can comprehend it.

11. At the close of chapter 8, we read,

> Then the king, and all Israel with him, offered sacrifice before the LORD. [63] Solomon offered as peace offerings to the LORD 22,000 oxen and 120,000 sheep. So the king and all the people of Israel dedicated the house of the LORD . . . [66] On the eighth day he sent the people away, and they blessed the king and went to their homes joyful and glad of heart for all the goodness that the LORD had shown to David his servant and to Israel his people. (1 Kgs 8:62–63, 66)

After God's glory enters the temple, Solomon, along with God's people bring sacrifices in such great quantity that the altar cannot hold them. The nation of Israel recognizes that as they participate in giving sacrifices to the Lord, they gain *atonement for their sins, forgiveness, salvation, and redemption.* In light of this wonderful day, the people are filled with joy and gladness, spawned by the knowledge of God's goodness to his people! What a day this must have been. I do not believe that words can completely capture the wonder of watching the glory of God fall down into the temple, while almost simultaneously finding the assurance that this holy God can be approached and satisfied by presenting to him the sacrifices he requires for the pardon and forgiveness of sins. No wonder God's people were so joyful!

As we summarize God's wonderful theocracy, we see a kingdom on earth that is characterized by the following attributes:

- Justice and righteousness
- Victory and dominion

- Peace and safety

- Wisdom

- Joy and happiness

- Wealth

- Nations seeking to see the glory of the king

- The temple and the worship of God

- The presence of the glory of God in the temple

- Sacrifices—assurance of atonement for sins, forgiveness, salvation, and redemption

The cumulative effect of all these characteristics is powerful, as reflected in Solomon's benediction found in 1 Kings 8:59–60, "Let these words of mine, with which I have pleaded before the LORD, be near to the LORD our God day and night, and may he maintain the cause of his servant and the cause of his people Israel, as each day requires, *60 that all the peoples of the earth may know that the Lord is God;* there is no other" (italics mine for emphasis). The significance of God's kingdom on earth—his theocracy—is that it might declare the glory of God to all the peoples on the entire earth! A close look at all of these attributes of the earthly kingdom of Israel under Solomon can only lead the reflective person to consider that this theocracy—this imperfect but glorious nation ruled by God through a king of his own choosing—is simply a miniature model or a momentary glimpse at a much greater kingdom and king to come! It is a glimpse into eternity!

From the day that the people of Israel left their slavery in Egypt, not knowing fully what God might do, to this glorious era of David and Solomon's kingly reigns in submission to their God, we have experienced a period of time of approximately four hundred and eighty years (1 Kgs 6:1). And if the seed promise was spoken to Abraham (and the patriarchs), and the law (or theocratic culture) was spoken to Moses, what literature might flow out of the height of the glorious days of David and Solomon? The answer is well-suited to the circumstances: poetry—expressions of the heart, as well as the full range of human emotions—joy, trust, hope, sorrow, struggle, confidence, etc.—along with thoughts of wisdom for all of life as it is lived in God's kingdom. The promise to Abraham is that God will make of him a great nation. Israel is a picture of God's people serving their God on earth. It is the fulfillment of the first big promise made by God to Abraham. It is also a temporary picture, of sorts, regarding the second big promise made to Abraham: that all the nations shall be blessed—that the world (of nations) shall be filled with the knowledge of the glory of God!

Written in the context of the apex of this glorious theocracy, Psalm 72, composed by Solomon, expresses God's goal in clear and optimistic terms,

"Give the king your justice, O God, and your righteousness to the royal son!

2 May he judge your people with righteousness, and your poor with justice!

3 Let the mountains bear prosperity for the people, and the hills, in righteousness!

4 May he defend the cause of the poor of the people, give deliverance to the children of the needy, and crush the oppressor!

6 May he be like rain that falls on the mown grass, like showers that water the earth!

7 In his days may the righteous flourish, and peace abound, till the moon be no more!

8 May he have dominion from sea to sea, and from the River to the ends of the earth!

11 May all kings fall down before him, all nations serve him!

12 For he delivers the needy when he calls, the poor and him who has no helper.

13 He has pity on the weak and the needy, and saves the lives of the needy.

14 From oppression and violence he redeems their life, and precious is their blood in his sight.

18 Blessed be the LORD, the God of Israel, who alone does wondrous things.

19 Blessed be his glorious name forever; *may the whole earth be filled with his glory!* Amen and Amen!" (Ps 72:1–4, 6–8, 11–14, 18–19; italics mine)

Indeed, may it be that the whole earth will be filled with the glory of God! And while it seems that, the nation of Israel—this grand and magnificent kingdom on earth—would be the perfect setting, and that now—the days of glorious theocracy—would be the perfect time, to send Jesus to reign, we are reminded that God's ways are not our ways, nor are God's thoughts our thoughts (Isa 55:8–9). God is at work and yet he works slowly. He works through people, people with a heart for God. He works in his own time. He starts small, takes the bad and makes it into good, and often chooses the hard way so that ultimately he gets the credit. One day, however, we can be reassured that "Jesus shall reign where'er the sun, does its successive journeys run, his kingdom stretch from shore to shore, till moons shall wax and wane no more!"[1]

Thus ends scene one in act one. We have observed eleven distinct steps, as God fulfills the first portion of his seed promise to Abraham. He has taken an aging man, married to a barren wife, and has blessed him with a nation that is more numerous than the stars in the sky or the sand on the shore. Is this progress? The Maasai tribe would affirm it! But they are also wondering, "What will happen next in God's great story of redemption?"

1. Watts, *Jesus Shall Reign*, Public Domain.

STEP 11

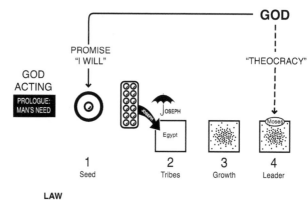

1	2	3	4
Seed	Tribes	Growth	Leader

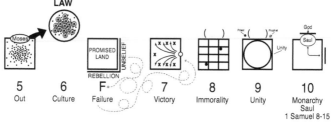

5	6	F	7	8	9	10
Out	Culture	Failure	Victory	Immorality	Unity	Monarchy Saul 1 Samuel 8-15

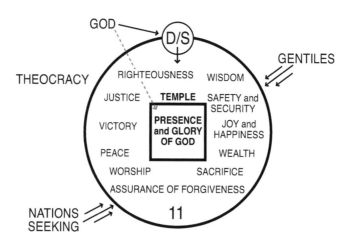

ACT ONE
SCENE ONE
SUMMARY

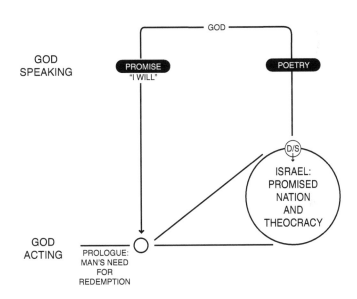

Act One, Scene Two

ACT ONE, SCENE ONE begins in Genesis chapter 12 and runs through 1 Kings chapter 10. We truly observe tremendous progress in God's redemptive program. I should remind us that we are watching God's progress in his redemptive plan by studying the historical timeline (God acting), which is the medium that supplies the unity of the Scriptures. We now arrive at scene two of the first act and that scene begins in 1 Kings.

In 1 Kings 11:1–6 we read these tragic words,

> Now King Solomon loved many foreign women, along with the daughter of Pharaoh: Moabite, Ammonite, Edomite, Sidonian, and Hittite women, ² from the nations concerning which the LORD had said to the people of Israel, "You shall not enter into marriage with them, neither shall they with you, for surely they will turn away your heart after their gods." Solomon clung to these in love. ³ He had 700 wives, who were princesses, and 300 concubines. And his wives turned away his heart. ⁴ For when Solomon was old his wives turned away his heart after other gods, and his heart was not wholly true to the LORD his God, as was the heart of David his father. ⁵ For Solomon went after Ashtoreth the goddess of the Sidonians, and after Milcom the abomination of the Ammonites. ⁶ So Solomon did what was evil in the sight of the LORD and did not wholly follow the LORD, as David his father had done.

In a few short verses and in a very brief verbal summary, we see the fall of the glorious theocracy. This fall is due to her king. Solomon is overwhelmed, not so much by the number of wives or concubines that he has married (many obtained through treaties made with the surrounding pagan nations), but by their idolatry. I once heard the late Roy Gustafson, longtime associate evangelist with the Billy Graham Evangelistic

Association, say that although Solomon has amassed a thousand wives and concubines, his biggest problem is having a thousand mother-in-laws! That thought is hilarious, but sadly, his biggest problem was loving these prized women so much that he lost his love for God. His heart of love for God was swayed toward the false gods and idols of pagans, so much so, that the text tells us that his dishonoring of the Lord was an act of evil! When we read Solomon's story, we should give pause to our own personal temptations toward creating idols, since those idols will similarly replace God in our own lives. He started so well, but he and the kingdom of Israel will not fare well due to his blatant sin!

The Lord is very angry with Solomon both because of his idolatry and because he has turned his heart away from the Lord. All of this, despite the fact that God has appeared before him twice, both times commanding him not to fall to the idolatry of the nations. Sadly, we read these words spoken to Solomon by the Lord and their import is staggering,

> Therefore the LORD said to Solomon, "Since this has been your practice and you have not kept my covenant and my statutes that I have commanded you, I will surely tear the kingdom from you and will give it to your servant. ¹² Yet for the sake of David your father I will not do it in your days, but I will tear it out of the hand of your son. ¹³ However, I will not tear away all the kingdom, but I will give one tribe to your son, for the sake of David my servant and for the sake of Jerusalem that I have chosen. (1 Kgs 11:11–13)

In just a few verses, we see God promise that he will tear the glorious kingdom from Solomon's hands. Note the sad refrain, one that had spawned hope in earlier days: "I will!" "I will" is mentioned five times in these three verses. God is promising that the kingdom, the nation that was formed to glorify his name to all the nations of the earth—the redemptive channel—is going to be dismantled. Even Solomon's own son will not rule the nation as it now exists.

Scene Two

Step One

Division

CHAPTER 11 OF 1 Kings explains the looming, tragic division of the kingdom of Israel. The text tells us the following story about Jeroboam, Solomon's son:

> The man Jeroboam was very able, and when Solomon saw that the young man was industrious he gave him charge over all the forced labor of the house of Joseph. ²⁹ And at that time, when Jeroboam went out of Jerusalem, the prophet Ahijah the Shilonite found him on the road. Now Ahijah had dressed himself in a new garment, and the two of them were alone in the open country. ³⁰ Then Ahijah laid hold of the new garment that was on him, and tore it into twelve pieces. ³¹ And he said to Jeroboam, "Take for yourself ten pieces, for thus says the LORD, the God of Israel, 'Behold, I am about to tear the kingdom from the hand of Solomon and will give you ten tribes ³² (but he shall have one tribe, for the sake of my servant David and for the sake of Jerusalem, the city that I have chosen out of all the tribes of Israel) . . . (1 Kgs 11:28–32)

Because of Solomon's sin, Israel will be torn into two nations, one consisting of ten tribes—the northern nation, known as Israel—and the other, the southern nation, consisting of only one tribe known as Judah. Jeroboam will be the king of the north. Furthermore, through Ahijah, the prophet, the Lord tells Jeroboam,

And I will take you, and you shall reign over all that your soul desires, and you shall be king over Israel. [38] And if you will listen to all that I command you, and will walk in my ways, and do what is right in my eyes by keeping my statutes and my commandments, as David my servant did, I will be with you and will build you a sure house, as I built for David, and I will give Israel to you. (1 Kgs 11:37–38)

This promise to Jeroboam appears to assure him that the Lord will have two theocratic nations, an amazing thought, but a sad one in light of the greatness of the former glorious theocracy.

In 1 Kings chapter 12, Rehoboam, who inherits his father Solomon's place as king over the southern kingdom (1 Kgs 11:43), lays heavy burdens upon the people of Israel, who thus lose their enthusiasm for and loyalty to him. Rehoboam desires to unite the northern and southern kingdoms, but the Lord sends a prophet, Shemaiah, who tells him not to fight the northern kingdom. He thus becomes king of one tribe, the southern kingdom, Judah. In the meantime, Jeroboam, in the north, becomes fully idolatrous, as he creates two golden calves for the people to worship, as well as high places for worship. He also conducts priestly duties himself as he offers sacrifices to the golden calves.

ACT ONE
SCENE TWO
STEP ONE:
KINGDOM SPLIT

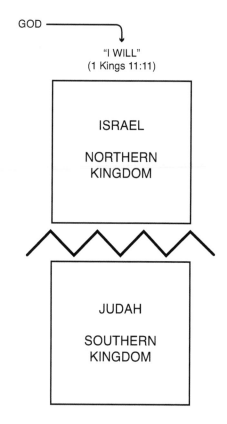

GOD

"I WILL"
(1 Kings 11:11)

ISRAEL

NORTHERN
KINGDOM

JUDAH

SOUTHERN
KINGDOM

Scene Two

Step Two

Fall of the Northern Kingdom

IN 1 KINGS CHAPTER 14, verses 7–9, we read that the prophet, Ahijah, goes to Jeroboam in the north and tells him that because of his rebellion, i.e., his evil idolatry, he has cast God behind his back. Therefore, God is going to cut off Jeroboam and his household (verse 10). In verses 14–15 we read,

> Moreover, the LORD will raise up for himself a king over Israel who shall cut off the house of Jeroboam today. And henceforth, [15] the LORD will strike Israel as a reed is shaken in the water, and root up Israel out of this good land that he gave to their fathers and scatter them beyond the Euphrates, because they have made their Asherim, provoking the LORD to anger. [16] And he will give Israel up because of the sins of Jeroboam, which he sinned and made Israel to sin.

God promises to strike Israel, the northern kingdom, and to scatter them beyond the Euphrates River. In time, God is going to raise up the nation of Assyria and wipe out his contumacious people! By the end of the chapter, Jeroboam is gone; his reign having lasted for twenty-two years.

Jereboam's sins of idolatry and rebellion are just the beginning of a practice that will be continued among a long line of the kings of Israel (the northern kingdom). Ultimately, we read that God's patience wears out, despite the fact that he constantly sends his messengers, the prophets, with appeals calling them to repent. In 2 Kings chapter 17, verses

6–8, we read these unbelievably tragic words describing the loss of the northern kingdom,

> In the ninth year of Hoshea, the king of Assyria captured Samaria, and he carried the Israelites away to Assyria and placed them in Halah, and on the Habor, the river of Gozan, and in the cities of the Medes. [7] And this occurred because the people of Israel had sinned against the LORD their God, who had brought them up out of the land of Egypt from under the hand of Pharaoh king of Egypt, and had feared other gods [8] and walked in the customs of the nations whom the LORD drove out before the people of Israel, and in the customs that the kings of Israel had practiced.

The Lord explains that he tried to persuade the people to return, but they would have none of it.

> Yet the LORD warned Israel and Judah by every prophet and every seer, saying, "Turn from your evil ways and keep my commandments and my statutes, in accordance with all the Law that I commanded your fathers, and that I sent to you by my servants the prophets." [14] But they would not listen, but were stubborn, as their fathers had been, who did not believe in the LORD their God. (2 Kgs 17:13–14)

God's anger swells because of the pagan behavior of his people and he judges them by extracting them from the land.

> And they abandoned all the commandments of the LORD their God, and made for themselves metal images of two calves; and they made an Asherah and worshiped all the host of heaven and served Baal. [17] And they burned their sons and their daughters as offerings and used divination and omens and sold themselves to do evil in the sight of the LORD, provoking him to anger. [18] Therefore the LORD was very angry with Israel and removed them out of his sight. None was left but the tribe of Judah only. (2 Kgs 17:16–18)

Israel, the northern kingdom, is now gone—finished, non-existent, abolished from the land by Sennacherib, king of Assyria. They have been removed from the sight of God and deservedly so! Their sins of idolatry that began through the leadership of Jereboam, as well as their termination by Assyria, is described in 2 Kings 17:21–23,

> When he had torn Israel from the house of David, they made Jeroboam the son of Nebat king. And Jeroboam drove Israel from

following the LORD and made them commit great sin. [22] The people of Israel walked in all the sins that Jeroboam did. They did not depart from them, [23] until the LORD removed Israel out of his sight, as he had spoken by all his servants the prophets. So Israel was exiled from their own land to Assyria until this day.

Step two in scene two of act one is the destruction and elimination of Israel. The northern kingdom no longer dwells in the Promised Land. The coming of *Assyria* as a vessel of God's wrath is *crisis "A"* in God's plan of redemption. And we are left to wonder, "Is this progress?"

ACT ONE
SCENE TWO
STEP TWO:

ISRAEL
REMOVED

CRISIS "A"
ASSYRIA

ISRAEL

JUDAH

Scene Two

Step Three

Fall of the Southern Kingdom

STEP THREE IN SCENE two of act one is sadly similar to step two. Although some of the kings of Judah (the southern kingdom, with its most significant city, Jerusalem) demonstrate repentance toward God, trigger spiritual revivals, and display both faith in and awe of the Lord, in time Judah succumbs to the same fate as Israel. In time, the Lord evaluates their behavior as worse than the surrounding pagan nations, which is truly saying something. Second Kings chapter 20 explains,

> And the LORD said by his servants the prophets, [11] "Because Manasseh king of Judah has committed these abominations and has done things more evil than all that the Amorites did, who were before him, and has made Judah also to sin with his idols, [12] therefore thus says the LORD, the God of Israel: Behold, I am bringing upon Jerusalem and Judah such disaster that the ears of everyone who hears of it will tingle. [13] And I will stretch over Jerusalem the measuring line of Samaria, and the plumb line of the house of Ahab, and I will wipe Jerusalem as one wipes a dish, wiping it and turning it upside down. [14] And I will forsake the remnant of my heritage and give them into the hand of their enemies, and they shall become a prey and a spoil to all their enemies, [15] because they have done what is evil in my sight and have provoked me to anger, since the day their fathers came out of Egypt, even to this day." (2 Kgs 21:10–15)

God promises such destruction of Judah and Jerusalem, that those who hear about it will have tingling ears. The picture of tingling ears speaks of ear aches, migraines, ringing ears, and numbness of hearing. God's judgment shall be great. The multiple usages of the phrase "I will" is harrowing! He further uses a second metaphor, that of wiping out a dish after being washed, a complete cleansing. And if the one washing the dish isn't certain that the cleaning is complete, the dish is taken in hand, wiped and turned upside down to insure that the rinsing and purifying is complete!

We read of this final step in the lengthy passage found in 2 Chronicles chapter 36.

> Zedekiah was twenty-one years old when he began to reign, and he reigned eleven years in Jerusalem. [12] He did what was evil in the sight of the LORD his God. He did not humble himself before Jeremiah the prophet, who spoke from the mouth of the LORD. [13] He also rebelled against King Nebuchadnezzar, who had made him swear by God. He stiffened his neck and hardened his heart against turning to the LORD, the God of Israel. [14] All the officers of the priests and the people likewise were exceedingly unfaithful, following all the abominations of the nations. And they polluted the house of the LORD that he had made holy in Jerusalem. [15] The LORD, the God of their fathers, sent persistently to them by his messengers, because he had compassion on his people and on his dwelling place. [16] But they kept mocking the messengers of God, despising his words and scoffing at his prophets, until the wrath of the LORD rose against his people, until there was no remedy. [17] Therefore he brought up against them the king of the Chaldeans, who killed their young men with the sword in the house of their sanctuary and had no compassion on young man or virgin, old man or aged. He gave them all into his hand. [18] And all the vessels of the house of God, great and small, and the treasures of the house of the LORD, and the treasures of the king and of his princes, all these he brought to Babylon. [19] And they burned the house of God and broke down the wall of Jerusalem and burned all its palaces with fire and destroyed all its precious vessels. [20] He took into exile in Babylon those who had escaped from the sword, and they became servants to him and to his sons until the establishment of the kingdom of Persia, [21] to fulfill the word of the LORD by the mouth of Jeremiah, until the land had enjoyed its Sabbaths. All the days that it lay desolate it kept Sabbath, to fulfill seventy years. (2 Chr 36:11–21)

This passage tells us that Zedekiah, the last king of Israel is not only evil, but he will not humble himself before God's messenger, the prophet Jeremiah. Furthermore, the king, the priests, and the people altogether follow the abominations of the surrounding nations, as well as dishonoring God's holy place, the temple. God has no relevance in their lives (a truly scary thought for any people and any generation). They continually mock God's prophets, to the point that God's wrath is so kindled that there is no remedy. God's answer is to judge not only Judah, but to destroy both Jerusalem and the temple. God will use the terrifying and evil nation of Babylon (also known as the Chaldeans; see the book of Habakkuk) to discipline his people. The people will be swept up like dust being vacuumed off the floor and scattered across the nation of Babylon to become enslaved inhabitants in a foreign land. God's city, God's people, God's temple, and shockingly, God's presence, as manifested by his glory in the temple, are *all gone!* The coming of *Babylon* as a vessel of God's wrath is crisis *"B"* in God's plan of redemption.

Scene two of act one can simply be entitled, "God's Wrath!" God judges his insubordinate and resistant people, a nation fully given over to evil, idolatry and rebellion against God. He disassembles and scatters his channel of redemption. Although covering many years of Israelite history, act one, scene two can be summarized by these three steps:

- Step One: The kingdom of God/channel of redemption is *split* into two kingdoms, northern (Israel) and southern (Judah)

- Step Two: The northern kingdom, Israel, is judged by God through the nation of Assyria. This is *Crisis "A"* (722 BC)

- Step Three: The southern kingdom, Judah, is judged by God through the nation of Babylon. This is *Crisis "B"* (586 BC)

Two major crises occur, resulting in the loss of God's channel of redemption. The once flourishing theocracy of Israel has been *crushed!* And in the midst of all of this judgment, we hear that the exile of the people of Israel, as prophesied by Jeremiah, will last for seventy years (Jer 29:10). So, we are absolutely compelled to ask this penetrating question, "Is there any progress occurring in scene two of act one?" Buck Hatch would find one consolation in this devastating chapter of Israel's history. In his own words, "One good thing came out of this—God sent the prophets. God wants us to understand the problems and the progress of the prophets!" He would contend that because there are two lengthy accounts of the ministry of the prophets (1 and 2 Kgs, 1 and 2 Chr), the historical context of the prophets' ministry in the times of royal failure is significant. I would agree with the esteemed Mr. Hatch. But, I would also like to propose that there is another element of progress that occurs in this period of disobedience, dismay, and utter disappointment. That element is that the need for a great, glorious, and God-centered king, i.e., a messiah who can deliver his people from their sins, has never been more evident. And he shall come! Human kings fail and they can fail miserably. As we listen to the words that God speaks through the voices of the prophets, we will hear many hints, with some being quite conspicuous, that such a king is coming to Israel. Truly, there has never been, nor will there ever be, a king like the king to come. Everything appears bleak now, but God is still at work. And that is progress![1]

Come, Thou long-expected Jesus,
Born to set Thy people free;
From our fears and sins release us,
Let us find our rest in Thee.
Israel's Strength and Consolation,
Hope of all the earth Thou art;
Dear Desire of every nation,
Joy of every longing heart.

Born Thy people to deliver,
Born a child and yet a King,
Born to reign in us forever,
Now Thy gracious kingdom bring.
By Thine own eternal Spirit
Rule in all our hearts alone;
By Thine all sufficient merit,
Raise us to Thy glorious throne.[2]

---

1. There is one other sign of "unseen" progress that occurs during this dark period, and it has to do with the scattering of the people across the Babylonian empire.

2. Wesley, *Come, Thou Long Expected Jesus*, Public Domain.

ACT ONE
SCENE TWO
STEP THREE:

JUDAH
REMOVED
(INTO
CAPTIVITY)

CRISIS "B"
BABYLON

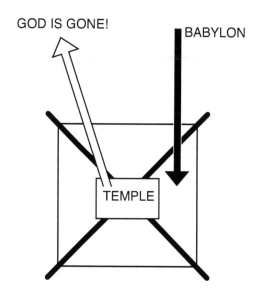

GOD IS GONE!

BABYLON

TEMPLE

GOD'S WRATH

ACT ONE
SCENES ONE AND TWO
SUMMARY

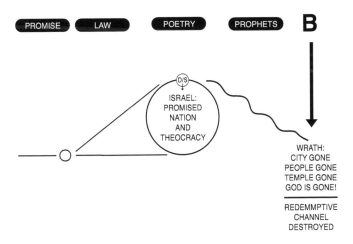

Act One, Scene Three

Matthew's Framework

In order to set the stage for scene three of act one, we need to take a brief look at Matthew chapter 1 where we read these phrases, shortened in order to make the point,

> ¹ The book of the genealogy of Jesus Christ, the son of David, the son of Abraham.

> ² Abraham was the father of Isaac, and Isaac the father of Jacob, and Jacob the father of Judah and his brothers, ³ and Judah the father of Perez . . . and Salmon the father of Boaz by Rahab, and Boaz the father of Obed by Ruth, and Obed the father of Jesse, ⁶ and Jesse the father of David the king. (Matt 1:1–3, 5–6a)

> ⁶ And David was the father of Solomon by the wife of Uriah, ⁷ and Solomon the father of Rehoboam, and Rehoboam the father of Abijah, and Abijah the father of Asaph . . . ¹¹ and Josiah the father of Jechoniah and his brothers, at the time of the deportation to Babylon. (Matt 1:6b–7, 11)

> ¹² And after the deportation to Babylon: Jechoniah was the father of Shealtiel, and Shealtiel the father of Zerubbabel . . . ¹⁶ and Jacob the father of Joseph the husband of Mary, of whom Jesus was born, who is called Christ. (Matt 1:12, 16)

If we notice the three names with which Matthew begins his gospel, we will better understand the breakdown of the genealogies. Of course those names are Jesus Christ, David, and Abraham. If we reverse those names—Abraham, David, and Jesus—as Matthew does next, we can see the chronological pattern that Matthew is creating. Notice that in doing so, our three scenes will arise:

- Scene One: Abraham to David the King
- Scene Two: David and Solomon, to the deportation to Babylon
- Scene Three: After the deportation to Babylon, to Joseph and Mary to whom Jesus was born

Matthew points out his rationale for writing the genealogies as he does. And of course, in doing so, he is trying to show the Jewish people of his day that not only can he trace Jesus back to Abraham, their father, but that Jesus is in the line of King David because he, himself, is a king, even their king, King of the Jews!

> ¹⁷ So all the generations from Abraham to David were fourteen generations, and from David to the deportation to Babylon fourteen generations, and from the deportation to Babylon to the Christ fourteen generations. (Matt 1:17)

Scene three is the bridge from the Old Testament to the New. The key historical books involved are Ezra, Nehemiah, and Esther. The setting for Ezra and Nehemiah is Jerusalem. The setting for Esther is Persia (formerly Babylon). In Ezra and Nehemiah, the power of God—God clearly at work—is obvious and wonderful. In the book of Esther, there is no mention of God. The book appears to avoid any explicit reference to God, although the providence and care of God shine forth for those who can see it.

Before we look at these three books, however, we need to remember that the people have been exiled for seventy years and God has been silent for that entire period as well. I do not think we can imagine what that silence on God's part would be like. I am reminded, however, of a story that helps us to understand the significance of seventy years of silence followed by a divine breakthrough. When my wife, Cathy, and I moved to Gainesville, Florida to do campus ministry at the University of Florida, we met an older woman who attended our church named Artie. Artie had walked with the Lord for many decades. Surprisingly, she "adopted" us almost immediately. It was like having a grandmother in our own city. Artie made us feel like the apple of her eye, feeding us at her home, bringing us unbelievable potato soup whenever we gave birth to one of our children, and slipping a twenty-dollar bill into my hand on occasion after a church service. Artie was fired up for the Lord and as I later discovered, she was known as "everyone's grandmother." At that point, that discovery was no epiphany. Nevertheless, her husband Paul was very unaffected by Artie's zeal for God. He was older than she was, but very laid back and seemingly totally disinterested in spiritual things. He almost never attended church. When I asked Artie about this, she explained that she married Paul when she was very young (mid-teenage years, as I recall) and although they both went to church originally, after they got married Paul lost all interest in religious matters. Artie, herself, became very distracted by life "in the world" as she tells it, but eventually she came back to the Lord. However, a harsh reality remained—decades passed with no apparent interest in the Lord on the part of Paul.

But one day, being in his early eighties, Paul became ill and was diagnosed with fluid on the heart. He lost all energy, was given both medicines and drug treatments that were supposed to help the fluid disappear, and was bedridden for quite some time. Cathy and I visited him a few times at their home. He could hardly speak, had no energy whatsoever, and lay in bed almost motionless. Weeks passed and amazingly, Paul's health improved. Once when we visited him, he said, "Please bring me some books to read about the Christian faith." I told him I would, so I went to my library and found some simple books on the Christian life and how to live for Christ. I gave them to Paul and in a matter of days he finished them. He then asked for a Bible. I gave him a modern English version and he began to read it every day. Eventually, enough of his strength returned and he told Artie, "I want to go to Faith Church!" He came three or four weeks in a row and then he said, "I need to go to the ear doctor and get new hearing aids. I want to hear the sermons!" Eventually, he became not only a constant attender of Faith Church, but he joined the older (mostly retired) members' weekly Bible study, and went to those meetings regularly as well. This transformation was amazing to watch and watch I did! Here was a man who lay spiritually dormant for sixty years or more and suddenly he was alive to everything about Christ! Possibly, of course, he had become converted to Christ, but whatever the explanation, it was incredible to observe! That change had to be something like what is about to happen to Israel, a nation that has been spiritually dormant and in exile for seven decades. Seventy years of nothing and silence on God's part (2 Chr 36:21), but then God intervenes! His grace and sovereignty prevail and the people are given hope. The channel of redemption is going to be restored.

Ezra/Nehemiah

God Working Powerfully

The text tells us,

> In the first year of Cyrus king of Persia, that the word of the Lord
> by the mouth of Jeremiah might be fulfilled, the Lord stirred up
> the spirit of Cyrus king of Persia, so that he made a proclamation
> throughout all his kingdom and also put it in writing: ² "Thus says
> Cyrus king of Persia: The Lord, the God of heaven, has given me
> all the kingdoms of the earth, and he has charged me to build him
> a house at Jerusalem, which is in Judah. ³ Whoever is among you
> of all his people, may his God be with him, and let him go up to
> Jerusalem, which is in Judah, and rebuild the house of the Lord,
> the God of Israel—he is the God who is in Jerusalem." (Ezra 1:1–3)

Suddenly, it seems, God is both speaking and working! He is raising up a
pagan king, Cyrus of Persia, to do his bidding. God's plan is to bring the
exiled people of Israel back to their land and to rebuild the temple there.
Upon viewing this event, we should find ourselves shouting "Hallelujah!"
The Maasai would be filled with wonder, hope, and if they dance, they
would be doing that too!

As we look at the books of Ezra and Nehemiah, we see that the plan of
both books is almost identical.

- Ezra has two sections, chapters 1–6 and then chapters 7–10.
- Nehemiah has two sections as well, chapters 1–6 and then
  chapters 7–13.

In Ezra chapter 1, we read that the house of God—the temple—is going to
be built (or rebuilt). This is huge! The focus of the first six chapters of Ezra
is upon the *building of the temple*! In chapter 2, a list is provided, naming
the exiles who are willing to return to their homeland. In chapter 3, we see
that the foundation of the temple is completed, along with much celebra-
tion of the people. Nevertheless, as we have learned, nothing comes easy
in God's kingdom and in chapter 4, the temple builders experience opposition from God's enemies. This chapter describes a period of discouragement
and the cessation of temple building. In chapter 5, the prophets Haggai and
Zechariah come upon the scene and encourage the builders in their task.
In chapter 6, we are told that the building is both completed and dedicated.
How wonderful is the progress that has been made—and this is progress!

Between chapters 6 and 7, a period of fifty to sixty years passes. In chapter 7, Ezra arrives. We are told, ". . . this Ezra went up from Babylonia. He was a scribe skilled in the Law of Moses that the LORD, the God of Israel, had given, and the king granted him all that he asked, for the hand of the LORD his God was on him" (Ezra 7:6). Ezra has come with the goal to teach the Lord's law, "For Ezra had set his heart to study the Law of the LORD, and to do it and to teach his statutes and rules in Israel" (Ezra 7:10, the summary verse for the second section of the book). In chapter 7, verses 23 and 25, we are told that King Artaxerxes commends Ezra and gives him the authority to re-establish God's way of life in Israel!

To summarize the progress seen in the book of Ezra, we read about the following positive events:

- The land is to be re-inhabited

- The people return to the land

- The temple is rebuilt

- Worship (the Passover) is reinstituted

- Revival (confession and repentance) takes place

- The law of God (the culture—God's way of life) is taught.

Ezra's two sections, stated in the simplest of categories, are: *house (temple)* and *law!* The book of Ezra contains a lot of progress!

Similarly, as noted above, Nehemiah contains two major sections, chapters 1–6 and chapters 7–13. Nehemiah, a true leader, arrives eleven years after Ezra's arrival. Chapter 1 of Nehemiah displays the motivation of Nehemiah to return to his homeland. Nehemiah lives in Susa, capital city of the Medo-Persian Empire, which is hundreds of miles away from Jerusalem. He hears of the plight of the city from one of his brothers and is particularly distressed that the people are in trouble, living in shame, and dwelling in a city of broken down walls. Nehemiah's kinsmen, those in Judah, live without protection from their enemies. Their living situation is precarious, as their lives are vulnerable to exposure and attack.

Living in a threatening and vulnerable setting is not easy to imagine. The best picture that I can paint to describe it (but one hardly as serious) is when Cathy and I visited some friends in south Florida in the 1980s. We had met this couple and their small children at a missions conference when we were raising funds for Reformed University Fellowship (RUF), our campus ministry at the University of Florida. After we got to know them, they invited us to stay at their new house (presently being built) the next time we came down for the church's missions conference (which was scheduled for the next year). We liked them a lot, both of us had young children, and we thought staying with them would be a great idea. When the conference arrived, we drove down to South Florida and arrived at their home which was located in a rather rural area inland, and a few miles west of the Atlantic coast. The wife welcomed us and told us that the newly constructed house was almost complete, except for one unfinished aspect. As she took us to our bedroom, she said, "The only thing we don't have in place yet are the doors. We have a door to our bedroom, but all the other bedrooms and bathrooms have no doors. We have put sheets over your bedroom door and over your bathroom door for your privacy." Of course, the fact that there were four or five small children between the two families left us very nervous about sleeping, showering, and using the bath facilities that weekend. We felt very vulnerable and nervous the entire time we stayed there.

Consider that situation in light of the fact that the Israelites, having settled in from their return from exile, are living in the midst of nations that are their enemies. Their enemies can walk right through the gaps in their walls, and intimidate/attack them. We can hardly imagine the discomfort that living daily in such a dangerous setting would bring us. Nehemiah weeps over their dilemma. In chapter 2, recognizing that God has put him in a position to make the request, he boldly and prayerfully asks the king (his employer) for permission to travel to Jerusalem. He returns, assesses the situation, and begins to rebuild the wall. Of course, once again, nothing comes easy in God's kingdom. Just like the builders of the temple foundation mentioned in the book of Ezra, Nehemiah and his builders face opposition, some of it intense and life threatening (chapter 2:10, and both chapters 4 and 6). However, in chapter 6, we are told, "So the wall was finished on the twenty-fifth day of the month Elul, in fifty-two days. [16] And when all our enemies heard of it, all the nations around us were afraid and fell greatly in their own esteem, for they perceived that this work had been accomplished with the help of our God" (Neh 6:15–16). Section one of Nehemiah is focused upon the building of the wall, a barrier that will bring both stability and security to the people of Israel.

Section two of Nehemiah describes the spiritual revival that takes place under the leadership of Nehemiah and the teaching ministry of Ezra. In a most stirring scene, the people gather to hear Ezra read the Book of the Law (Neh 8:8). In response, they celebrate the long forgotten feast of booths (Lev

23:33ff.), and corporately confess their sins and the sins of their fathers with much repentance, while making commitments (a covenant) to follow the Lord. The latter portion of the book describes Nehemiah's radical reforms as he deals with spiritual regressions (backsliding) of the people.

In essence, the book of Nehemiah's two sections, stated in the simplest of categories, are: *wall* and *revival!* The books of Ezra and Nehemiah contain a lot of progress! Together, both books bring the readers much encouragement. Their combined impact demonstrates the power of God in doing one thing: *rebuilding his nation.* What was once lost has now been recreated. We see the following major accomplishments mentioned in these two records:

- Land regained

- People (a remnant) return

- The house of God (the temple) rebuilt

- The law (the way of life) restored

- The wall is rebuilt, leading to security and peace

What has God done in these two significant books? *He has restored his channel of redemption on earth!* This is progress!

SCENE THREE

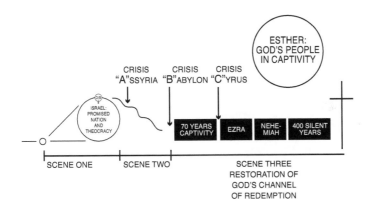

EZRA		NEHEMIAH	
LAND PEOPLE TEMPLE WORSHIP	LAW (Way of Life)	LEADER WALL (Security)	REVIVAL and REFORMATION
1-6	7-10	1-6	7-13

WHY IS CRISIS "C" A CRISIS?
1. THE PEOPLE ARE ONLY A REMNANT (EZRA 9:8)
2. THE PEOPLE OF GOD ARE IN BONDAGE/SLAVERY (EZRA 9:8-9)
3. THE GLORY OF GOD IS ABSENT (UNWRITTEN)

Differences

However, we need to explore the answer to this probing question: What is the difference between this nation and the theocracy that existed prior to the exile? The answer is found in Ezra 9:8–9,

> But now for a brief moment favor has been shown by the LORD our God, to leave us a remnant and to give us a secure hold within his holy place, that our God may brighten our eyes and grant us a little reviving in our slavery. [9] For we are slaves. Yet our God has not forsaken us in our slavery, but has extended to us his steadfast love before the kings of Persia, to grant us some reviving to set up the house of our God, to repair its ruins, and to give us protection in Judea and Jerusalem.

Firstly, the people who populate the land are only a remnant, i.e., a mere shadow of what the glorious Jerusalem once was. Approximately fifty thousand people returned to Jerusalem. The majority of God's people remain scattered. They are dispersed because of their rebellion. Secondly, the people of God are in bondage; they are in subjection to the Gentiles. Nehemiah reinforces this stark reality when he writes, "Behold, we are slaves this day; in the land that you gave to our fathers to enjoy its fruit and its good gifts, behold, we are slaves. [37] And its rich yield goes to the kings whom you have set over us because of our sins. They rule over our bodies and over our livestock as they please, and we are in great distress" (Neh 9:36–37). The bondage of God's people begins with Assyria, reaches epic proportions with Babylon, continues with the Medo-Persian empire, and in coming years, they will remain underneath both Greece and Rome. This historical situation doesn't change—bondage becomes a lasting state for God's people. With these realities in perspective, Buck Hatch expresses the thought that, although it is unwritten, saddest of all is the fact that the glory of God is absent. Members of the Maasai tribe must wonder, "Will God's glory ever return to his people again?"

"The Place"

In so many ways, scene three is very exciting! We are watching the power of God in restoring his people to the land. But as exciting as these events appear to us, we are compelled to ask, "Why is the channel of redemption being restored? Even though the channel of redemption has been modified, what factors seem to bring it to pass?" To answer these questions, we must briefly look at some key scripture passages, two in the Old Testament and one in the New Testament. Deuteronomy chapter 12 provides needed insight for us. In this chapter, we find multiple references to "the place." Speaking of the lure of false worship, Moses tells the next generation that when they arrive in "the land," they must destroy the places where the nations engage in worshiping their idols. Then he writes,

> You shall not worship the LORD your God in that way. [5] But you shall seek *the place* that the LORD your God will choose out of all your tribes to put his name and make his habitation there. There you shall go, [6] and there you shall bring your burnt offerings and your sacrifices, your tithes and the contribution that you present, your vow offerings, your freewill offerings, and the firstborn of your herd and of your flock. (Deut 12:4–6, italics mine for emphasis)

We also read references in Deuteronomy chapter 12 to "the place" in verses 11, 13, 14, 18, 21, and 26. "The place" is Jerusalem. Jerusalem is "the place" of sacrifice. According to verse 13, there is no other place to bring one's offerings to God but "the place." Jerusalem is the place chosen by God for true worship!

Psalm 137 is a psalm written about the experience of the exiles in Babylon. In their captivity, they remember Zion, which is a designation for the city of Jerusalem. They are homesick and heartsick for Zion and cannot sing any of the Lord's songs because they are in a foreign land. Their captors sarcastically mock them by requesting songs of Zion. Why are they in a foreign land instead of their homeland? Because of their rebellion. God is gone from "the place" and they have been removed from "the place," the place of worship and praise.

In the gospel of John, chapter 4, we listen in on Jesus's conversation with the Samaritan woman at the well. Deflecting Jesus's penetrating questions into her personal life, she changes the subject, asking about the proper place for worship of God. She comments, "Sir, I perceive that you are a prophet. [20] Our fathers worshiped on this mountain, but you say that in Jerusalem is the place where people ought to worship" (John 4:19–20). Even in Jesus's day, Jerusalem is known as "the place" of worship.

In Babylon, the exiles built synagogues in order to gather for worship. Apparently, they prayed toward Jerusalem from those synagogues. In 2 Chronicles 6:34–35, we read, "If your people go out to battle against their enemies, by whatever way you shall send them, and they pray to you toward this city that you have chosen and the house that I have built for your name, [35] then hear from heaven their prayer and their plea, and maintain their cause" (see also 1 Kings 8:28–30). Pray toward Jerusalem! We see this practice carried out by Daniel as well, "When Daniel knew that the document had been signed, he went to his house where he had windows in his upper chamber *open toward Jerusalem*. He got down on his knees three times a day and prayed and gave thanks before his God, as he had done previously" (Dan 6:10, italics mine).

Why is "the place" being restored? Why is the channel of redemption being recovered and reestablished? The answer is profound—Christ must be sacrificed in Jerusalem! Buck Hatch contends, "There is no other place on earth where men might be saved, but in Jerusalem!" Jerusalem is "the place" to which God will send his son to be a sacrifice for the sins of the world! Jerusalem is the place of worship. In the Old Testament, the people of Israel look forward by faith to the work of atonement that will take place in the temple of Jerusalem, even the Holy of Holies. Daniel prayed toward Jerusalem, even though the city had been destroyed. Jerusalem was God's holy city and the place where men and women could "get right with God." In the book of Ezra, when the people return to Jerusalem, the first thing they do is build an altar. The altar precedes the temple. The altar is the place where people get in touch with God! In Amos 3:2, we read, "You only have I known of all the families of the earth . . ." God only knows the Jews and they only know him through the sacrificial system, where atonement (getting right with God) occurs. In the books of Ezra and Nehemiah, God's power is wonderfully displayed as "the place" for sacrifice is being restored! This is progress that eventually will provide the height of progress in God's grand redemptive plan!

Esther

As we turn our attention to Esther, we recognize that God has his people in two different places. The book of Esther is the first time in the development of Scripture that there is a book (a list or a record) describing God's covenant people outside of the land. Why? Because this is the first time that they have been dispersed in bondage. Here is a quick review of the book of Esther:

- Chapters 1–3: The Jews are endangered

- Chapters 4–10: The Jews are delivered

The drama of Esther has such a thrilling plot as it unfolds, that the novice reader (think Maasai!) should not be able to put the book down.

The scenario of the situation is provided in Esther 3:8, "Then Haman said to King Ahasuerus, 'There is a certain people scattered abroad and dispersed among the peoples in all the provinces of your kingdom. Their laws are different from those of every other people, and they do not keep the king's laws, so that it is not to the king's profit to tolerate them.'" Esther 1:1 tells us that there are one hundred and twenty-seven provinces in the Medo-Persian empire, stretching from India to Ethiopia. "These people"—the Jews—are everywhere! Haman notes, with disdain, that this "certain people" are people living according to God's laws. These people are called Jews over forty different times in the book (they are no longer viewed as "the people of the most-high God"). The phrase "Jew" is not a compliment—it is an ethnic stereotype. God is obviously working in the books of Ezra and Nehemiah, but there is no mention of God's name in the book of Esther.

However, in seven different instances, we read passages that imply *God's providence*:

- Esther 2:9 "And the young woman pleased him and won his favor." (Speaking of the king—Ahasuerus—who was parading various women, in a beauty pageant fashion, in order to find a replacement for his upstart wife, Vashti.)

- Esther 2:15 "Now Esther was winning favor in the eyes of all who saw her." (God granting his favor and providential care to Esther through the onlookers.)

- Esther 2:17 ". . . the king loved Esther more than all the women, and she won grace and favor in his sight more than all the virgins, so that he set the royal crown on her head and made her queen instead of Vashti." (Another reference to the king's favor toward Esther; ultimately, it is an expression of God's favor toward Esther.)

- Esther 4:14 "For if you keep silent at this time, relief and deliverance will rise for the Jews from another place, but you and your father's house will perish." (A statement made by Esther's uncle Mordecai, who believes that "God" will provide another way to save his people.)

- Esther 4:14 "And who knows whether you have not come to the kingdom for such a time as this?" ("Such a time" is a phrase speaking of God's providential timing.)

- Esther 4:16 "Go, gather all the Jews to be found in Susa, and hold a fast on my behalf, and do not eat or drink for three days, night or day. I and my young women will also fast as you do." (Fasting, with God implied, rather than prayer.)

- Esther 4:16 "Then I will go to the king, though it is against the law, and if I perish, I perish." (Esther casts herself and her life in the hands of a providential God.)

Throughout the entire book, there is no reference to anything connected to God, certainly not by name. So, we wonder, "Why?" We might think that the people don't know about God; but, there is a remnant that does, so that is not the answer. We might surmise that these Hebrew exiles don't want to bring offense to their captors based upon their religion. But, we do see Daniel stand up for both God and his faith. By inference, it appears that the answer is related to both Jerusalem and the temple. As mentioned above, God chose to put this name in Jerusalem. He does work in "the place"—Jerusalem—but apparently, he does not work in the same manner for those who live in captivity. As exiles, because of their sin and rebellion, God's "voice of power" remains silent. God does not always work powerfully in every situation in the Old Testament. He is working supernaturally in Jerusalem and Israel, but outside of Jerusalem, he is working through his providence. He uses natural circumstances to put his will into effect. In Ezra and Nehemiah—God is working in power. But in Esther, it "just happened" that,

- The king disposes of his wife, Queen Vashti

- The king chooses Esther as his queen

- The king couldn't sleep—he must do something for Mordecai

- Esther's request before the king is granted

Clearly, God's providence is displayed throughout the narrative of the book. God's providence is not his supernatural power, but his working out of all circumstances by his sovereign guidance. Buck Hatch speaks of God's "right hand of power" and his "left hand of providence." Ezra, Nehemiah, and Esther manifest the use of both of God's hands in the lives of his people.

So, once again, we must ask the question: what is the relevance of the book of Esther? Why is it included in the historical narrative of God's redemptive plan if God does not speak, is not mentioned, and appears in his providence only? The short answer is that Haman was an evil, jealous man who wanted to kill all of the Jews. His hope was to wipe them out completely. Haman is a picture of Satan, who is always opposing the redemptive plan of God. Satan is using Haman to obliterate God's people who are living in exile. Esther is used by God to deliver his people. Through

Esther's courageous efforts (although she does not initially reveal that she is a Jew), the king favors her and makes a new law, "The Jews can defend themselves!" God's people are delivered from their peril. They are delivered by a providential act of God. They withstand this threat. But they will continue in bondage, as they also exist in the future, living under the domains of both Greece and Rome. But, they survive to see another day. Why? God is going to use them later on in history. According to history, God's people remain in both the Promised Land and scattered in captivity, while living underneath the authority of pagan nations and rulers. Unfortunately, the majority of them continue to live in defiance of God's will for their lives, as it was revealed to them in the Torah. Malachi, the last prophet that God sends to his wayward people, explains the obstinate and heartless manner of living that exists among God's people during his days. Because of their condemnation and God's utter disgust with their behavior, God ceases to speak to or work on their behalf. And based upon their disobedience, he remains silent for an unbelievable period lasting four hundred years. The Maasai are wondering, "Will God ever help his people again? Does he still love them? Does he care enough to do something for a people who will not listen to or obey his voice? What will happen next? What might be the rest of the story?"

Four hundred years of silence! In our world today, we can hardly go forty seconds without sound or communication of some sort. Silence—we rarely seek it out. Yet the Lord is so exacerbated with the nation of Israel that he stops speaking and he also stops acting. He sends no prophets to call them back to the way of godliness. He does no miracles or acts of providence on their behalf. Four hundred years without God intervening in some significant manner is quite unbelievable. God is quiet.

SCENE THREE
CAPTIVITY

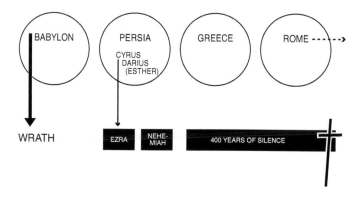

EZRA/NEHEMIAH - GOD'S POWER (REDEMPTIVE CHANNEL RESTORED)
ESTHER - GOD'S PROVIDENCE (GOD'S PEOPLE PRESERVED)

God Has a Plan

But God has a plan. It is a plan of redemption and salvation for his people. It is a plan for the world! God promised Abraham that he would make of him (an elderly man with a barren wife, i.e., a childless couple) into a great nation. That promise was fulfilled through the eventual building of a theocracy, a nation led by God through God's man. And that theocracy was Israel. Yet God made a second promise to Abraham; that promise is an assurance that he would bless the entire world through Abraham's seed. And in time, the Lord will reach his goal for the earth: that all of the earth shall be filled with the knowledge of the glory of God as the waters cover the sea!

However, at the end of the Old Testament, the channel of God's redemptive plan appears to have faded into insignificance. The nation of Israel is found to be living in bondage to a number of major world nations for a number of centuries. As a nation, their spiritual well-being has decayed in such a manner that, in the early first century, most of their spiritual leaders conform to a form of external spirituality but are missing a heart for God. A remnant awaits a promised messiah who will come and set them free from their captivity. Who could have hope for any spiritual breakthrough after four hundred years of silence on God's part? Will anything ever happen?

God Acts

The messiah (the anointed deliverer) will come. God is going to act! The coming of the messiah is part of God's plan to act in history. God promises (he speaks) and he delivers (he acts). The Apostle Paul writes in his letter to the Galatian Christians, "But when the fullness of time had come, God sent forth his Son, born of woman, born under the law, [5] to redeem those who were under the law, so that we might receive adoption as sons" (Gal 4:4–5). The phrase "the fullness of time" indicates that God has sent his son, Jesus, at the perfect time—it was God's time. It was the world's time! God does something so big, at the time when it was so needed, that we cannot fully comprehend it. What did God *do*? Paul explains, "For in him all the fullness of God was pleased to dwell . . ." (Col 1:19). God became man, one of us, yet without sin. The incarnation (God becoming an actual human, in the flesh, yet without sin) is one of the most incredible facts and acts in history that the world has ever known or seen! What else did God *do* in sending his son? He reconciled the world to himself. Again Paul states, ". . . in Christ God was reconciling the world to himself, not counting their trespasses against them, and entrusting to us the message of reconciliation" (2 Cor 5:19). When we remember that it is history (or God acting) that unifies the Bible, we begin to understand how big it is that the central focus of history is found in God sending his redeemer son, Jesus Christ. The fullness of God has come down to earth in the flesh that, through his death on the cross, we might turn from our sins and become friends with God!

God Speaks

But in Christ, God not only acts—he speaks! The author of the book of Hebrews begins by writing, "Long ago, at many times and in many ways, God spoke to our fathers by the prophets, [2] but in these last days *he has spoken to us by his Son*, whom he appointed the heir of all things, through whom also he created the world" (Heb 1:1–2, italics mine). Just prior to the appearance of Jesus as a baby, God sends his messengers, the angels, into the world to announce the coming birth of his son. Whenever these angels do appear, it is as if they have been trained in the heavenly school of angels to declare, "Do not fear!" Angelic appearances and other interventions by God have not occurred in four centuries, so it is only natural that when an angel shows up as a radiant, holy messenger with good news from the living God, the recipients would be terrified! God is once again speaking to his people and getting ready to speak more loudly than he ever has. "This is my beloved Son; listen to him!" (Mark 9:7). To whom are we listening? Isaiah 9:6 describes Jesus as the "Wonderful Counselor." Matthew 7:28–29 states, "And when Jesus finished these sayings, the crowds were astonished at his teaching, [29] for he was teaching them as one who had authority, and not as their scribes." No one ever has spoken or will speak like Jesus speaks!

If the Bible can be divided into two aspects of revelation, i.e., God acting (history) and God speaking (doctrine and teaching), then Jesus fulfills both. Jesus Christ is God acting in this world and God speaking to the world. When we speak of God revealing himself, Jesus, the messiah, is both—what God *says* and what God *does*! How does Jesus compare with all of history? There is no comparison. Jesus is the greatest thing that God has ever done or said. History revolves around Jesus! God the Father sent God the Son to speak to us and to act on our behalf. Behold him and listen to him. Don't miss Jesus! Believe in him and receive him as your own!

The coming of Jesus as messiah is not only the greatest thing God has ever done or said, but Christ is *the culmination of everything preceding or following his coming*! Jesus is the foundation of everything that happens in history. If the cross of Christ falls, everything else in the Scriptures fall. It goes beyond personal salvation. It goes beyond organized religion and the church. It goes beyond Christian tradition. If Jesus isn't God speaking and acting with the loudest effect possible at the cross of Calvary, then the Bible means nothing. And how loud is the resurrection? Sonic boom loud!

And how do we know that Jesus is God both speaking and acting? In his redemptive plan, God underscores the magnitude of his deafening message by giving us four historical records of his son—both his words and his work. The four gospels are like four exclamation points in the historical record of scripture. Matthew, Mark, Luke, and John!!!! We hear God telling us the story of his son with a quadruple emphasis. Four accounts of one marvelous drama! Can we hear God? Matthew, Mark, Luke, and John = Jesus Christ is everything!

As I think of the four gospels, I am reminded of a cute story that happened to Cathy and I back in 1981. We were about to have our first child and the cultural rage in having babies at that time was a procedure known as the Lamaze method of natural childbirth. We decided that natural childbirth, with the husband as a coach during the birthing process, was a great idea. So, we signed up for a class being held at the Shands Teaching Hospital of the University of Florida. The class involved six meetings in which we learned about Lamaze. Including ourselves, there were eight couples attending the sessions. Those sessions were led by a very capable and veteran instructor, an OB/GYN nurse named Audrey, who had taught the course for many years. She was the consummate professional and, as I recall, the head of obstetrics/gynecology nursing at Shands. At the very last meeting of the training, it was obvious that Audrey had planned a motivational session for all of the couples who attended. We didn't walk through any further training or practice any coaching. Nor did we have any instruction. Audrey explained that she believed we were all well prepared to go through the natural childbirth process. For the evening's meeting, she had invited two different couples who had been through the course previously and experienced very successful Lamaze-based childbirths. These couples were strategically presented to us. The first couple was, like ourselves and most of the attendees, in their mid-twenties. There could not have been a more perfect and polished couple chosen to present their successful natural childbirth than this husband and wife. They were very attractive. Both were articulate, well-educated, and professional. The husband was in graduate school at the University of Florida and both of them had attended a major university, gaining undergraduate degrees. They were dressed in a collegiate, casual, but preppy style (I told Cathy that I was sure they attended Auburn University as undergraduates), had perfect teeth, and could have been models for high-end fashion magazines. They gave their story, baby in arms, filled with smiles and confidence. Listening to them, we felt certain that we could do the same.

However, just in case there might be some couple in the group who was not certain of their capability, Audrey had devised the most convincing testimony possible. What I am about to tell you is a true story, although you might not believe me when I am done. After the polished couple finished speaking, Audrey asked another couple to come into the room. Standing side by side, they were almost the opposite of the first couple. They were very "country," having driven twenty or so miles outside of Gainesville to come to the meeting. They were "salt of the earth" (or we call it "down home" in the south) native Floridians who had grown up in a small town setting nearby. Very rural, they were clean, but wore somewhat homely, out-dated clothing. They had strong, southern accents and it was not apparent that either of them had any education beyond high school. They were not particularly physically fit and I don't think either of them had all of their teeth. Yet, they were very happy, positive, enthusiastic, and proud as could be to tell their own story. Amazingly, it seemed, they told us that they had given birth to four boys using the Lamaze technique. And the mother was beaming as she held the most recent boy, probably less than three months old, in her arms. It seemed very obvious that Nurse Audrey was communi-cating to all of us that if this couple could pull off the Lamaze method four different times, then *anyone* could do it. That was not stated, but simply implied. They were such a humble and cheery couple that everyone in the room gave them their attention as they told their story.

After both couples finished, Audrey thanked the two presenting couples and turned to the group, making the inevitable inquiry, "Are there any questions?" Of course, the hour was late and everyone there was ready to go home and prepare to have their babies. Nevertheless, one of the wives raised her hand, which was a surprise to all of us. Nurse Audrey recognized her and asked her to present her question. It was the only ques-tion of the evening. I was sure it would be some sort of heavy medical type question, but I was wrong. This Lamaze participant was personally far more interested in the presenting couples than I was. She turned to the "country" couple and asked, "You said that you had four sons doing the Lamaze method. What are your boys' names?" (You cannot make this up!) The mother was beaming with pride to be asked—let's face it, hav-ing four children through natural childbirth is quite the accomplishment. She enthusiastically answered, with an angelic look on her face, "My boys' names are Matthew, Mark, Luke, (then holding up her most recent baby boy in her arms, she exuberantly declared) and this is Fred!" Yes, Matthew, Mark, Luke, and—Fred! Amazingly, no one in the crowd, except Cathy and I, who had to squash our surprised laughter, seemed to notice the incongruity. We're not sure what happened to John, the fourth gospel boy's name, and we didn't ask. A friend of ours surmised that maybe this was the last boy they were planning to have and beloved Uncle Fred had recently passed away. We will never know. But when it comes to God sending his son to die for the world, the Father underscores the significance of this act.

He solemnly declares it by recording the event using four different testimonies. These four testimonies, taken together, are powerful witnesses to what God was doing in and through his divine son, Jesus Christ! And as C.S. Lewis once stated describing the Gospel witness of the Scriptures, "I have been reading poems, romances, vision literature, legends, and myths all my life. I know what they are like. I know none of them are like this. Of this [gospel] text there are only two possible views. Either this is reportage . . . or else, some unknown [ancient] writer . . . without known predecessors or successors, suddenly anticipated the whole technique of modern novelistic realistic narrative."[1] God is reporting an amazing and real story—the coming of his beloved Son, the messiah, and sacrifice for our sins. God is both speaking and acting, loudly and clearly! Matthew, Mark, Luke, and *John*—God asks, "Are you listening?"

1. Keller, *Reason*, 106.

Jesus, the End of Act One

JESUS IS THE CULMINATION of everything that precedes his coming, as seen in act one of God's redemptive drama. The four gospel accounts attempt to show us that the testimony of Jesus's birth, life, death, and resurrection is the monumental culmination of what God was doing in redemptive history. Jesus's life and death go far beyond the Old Testament system of law and sacrifice. He fulfills the moral law by keeping it perfectly and he is the fulfillment of the ceremonial law (the sacrificial system) by becoming an unblemished sacrifice that is given as a substitute (shedding his blood on the cross) for the sins of the world (both Jew and Gentile.)

How do we know that Jesus is the consummation of God's redemptive plan? Because God tells us. The writer of Hebrews clearly states,

> For Christ has entered, not into holy places made with hands, which are copies of the true things, but into heaven itself, now to appear in the presence of God on our behalf. [25] Nor was it to offer himself repeatedly, as the high priest enters the holy places every year with blood not his own, [26] for then he would have had to suffer repeatedly since the foundation of the world. But as it is, he has appeared once for all at the end of the ages to put away sin by the sacrifice of himself. (Heb 9:24–26)

Jesus appeared "*at the end* of the ages" (italics mine, for emphasis). He is the culmination of the plan of God! He is not just another step in the plan—he is the plan and his work on the cross is the end of the redemptive plan! And when he fulfills his part of the plan, he has completed the course that God the Father wants him to complete.

Hebrews 1:1–2 says, "Long ago, at many times and in many ways, God spoke to our fathers by the prophets, [2] but in these last days he has spoken to us by his Son, whom he appointed the heir of all things, through whom also he created the world." The author of Hebrews says that the spoken revelation of God through his Son is done in "these last days." The word "last" can mean "at the end" or "final." He is addressing the fact that Christ's coming was the *close* of these last days, i.e., the end of the days of God's plan of redemption.

Similarly, in 1 Peter, chapter 1, we read,

> . . . knowing that you were ransomed from the futile ways inherited from your forefathers, not with perishable things such as silver or gold, [19] but with the precious blood of Christ, like that of a lamb without blemish or spot. [20] He was foreknown before the foundation of the world but was *made manifest in the last times* for the sake of you . . . (1 Pet 1:18–20, italics mine)

Like the author of Hebrews, Peter speaks of Christ's redemptive work as being manifested in "the last times" or "in the end times." The triune God: Father, Son, and Holy Spirit, has *accomplished* the plan of redemption. God has chosen the recipients of redemption. Christ, the Son, has paid the purchase price for those recipients. And the Holy Spirit will apply the work of Christ to those whom God, the Father, has chosen. Most significant in making this point are the words that Jesus proclaims just before his death on the cross. Those poignant words are these, "It is finished!" (John 19:30). Then, as he expires, he says, "Father, into your hands I commit my spirit!" (Luke 23:46). The words, "it is finished," are spoken in regard to the amazing redemptive plan of God the Father. Christ's death is the end, even the culmination of God's plan, although, as we will see later, it is not the end but just the beginning. Nevertheless, it is the end of the unfolded plan of God to save the world. Christ finished his perfect work on the behalf of sinners.

God always works through a man. Jesus, the divine and eternal Son of God, became a man to do the Father's will. He died on behalf of his people and he had to become a man to do so. The incarnation (Christ— God the Son—becoming a flesh-and-blood human being) is the basis of all that God has ever done. Dr. J. I. Packer contends that the incarnation is bigger than the resurrection![1] This is why we believe in Christ, even when we cannot figure everything out about life, God, the future, or today! Christ is the center of history. On the road to Emmaus, as recorded in Luke 24, Jesus speaks with two inquisitive disciples and explains that the Old Testament is a story that continuously points to the coming mes-

---

1. Packer, *Knowing God*, 53.

siah. He interprets the text of Scripture to show them that from Genesis to Calvary, the story is about himself, Jesus, the messiah!

If we look at various Old Testament Scriptures and compare them with selective New Testament passages, we will see potential examples of what Jesus was telling the disciples on the road to Emmaus. Everything in both the Old and New Testaments, points to Jesus! Below are some selected Scripture passages demonstrating how all of the Bible testifies of Christ.

Prologue

Genesis 1: Creation → Christ, the creator God—John 1:3; Colossians 1:16-17

Genesis 2: Creation of man (humankind) → Christ, a man—1 Timothy 2:5; Hebrews 2:9

Genesis 3: The First Adam/Sin → Christ, the Last Adam—Romans 5:12; 1 Corinthians 15:54

Promise

Genesis 12: Abraham, Father of the Jews → Christ, a Jew/Abraham's Seed—Galatians 3:16

Law

Exodus 20: The Moral Law (10 Commandments) → Christ fulfills the law—Matthew 5:17;

Leviticus 4, 5, 7: The Ceremonial Law → Christ, fulfills the ceremonial law—Hebrews 10:1-14

History

Joshua 3:14-17 "Yahweh is salvation"—he leads God's people into victory (the Promised Land) → Jesus is salvation—he is the victor over sin and death and leads us into the heavenly promised land—1 Corinthians 15:56-57

Judges 2:16–18—Judges/saviors deliver God's people from their enemies → Christ saves us from our enemies: Satan, sin, and death—Luke 1:67–71

Poetry

Proverbs 8:1, 12–18; 8:34–35—"I, wisdom . . ." → Christ, in whom are all of the treasures of wisdom—Colossians 2:3

Prophets

Isaiah 53—The suffering messiah → The prophets predict the suffering of Christ—1 Peter 1:10–11

Church History

Acts 4:10-12—"Preach Jesus!"

The Epistles

Colossians 1:17–18—"He is the head of the body, the church"

Ephesians 4:4, 12—"There is one body . . ." The church is the body of Christ

Apocalyptic (Consummation)

Revelation 5:8-9—"Worthy is the Lamb . . ."

We could cite many, many other Scripture verses to demonstrate that the entire Bible testifies to Jesus Christ, the Son of God. The Old Testament testifies to the redeemer, the one who would come to save his people from their sins. He will build his church, a group of chosen people, consisting of Jew and Gentile, who will tell the world about their redeemer. Why? So that the knowledge of God's glory might fill the earth as the waters cover the sea! God is at work and his plan will not fail. The Massai wonder, "How will it happen?"

To be continued . . .

Conclusion

In the 1960s my Uncle John's piles of rubble, stones and rock, I-beams, and mounds of dirt became an indescribable mansion as various laborers put together seemingly incongruous materials to create one amazing edifice. We used to joke that my Uncle John must have put the carpenter's three children through college, because this extraordinarily gifted artisan, who could do anything with a piece of wood, worked on the house for a number of years! We were confident that he was paid handsomely. The finished product was quite impressive, and I was happy to see the entire work come together. From a child's vantage point, I did not see the forthcoming end product, but when completed it was a wonder. I used to bring my friends home from college and take them on tours of the entire house. I knew it well and no one was ever disappointed to see this marvelous residence firsthand.

We have watched God's plan of redemption unfold before our eyes. Although the Bible certainly seems mysterious, puzzling, and bewildering at times, we have gained a glimpse into the very heart of God. God watches the first Adam, along with his wife, Eve, fall to the seduction of the archenemy of our souls, Satan, who beguiles our first parents through the use of a serpent and the fruit of a sacred tree. The good and wonderfully created world, as it was once known, goes from very good to a state of wickedness and continual evil. Mankind balks against the call and will of God to fill the earth with his glory, but all is not lost. God has a plan! Through Abraham, he makes a promise—to make of one man (and his barren wife) a great nation, and through that man to bless the entire earth! Seemingly impossible, we see that all things are possible with God.

Ultimately, through multiple obstacles, including the frequent sins and failures of his people, the Lord does build a nation, a theocracy. Israel is a nation that will bring forth, though briefly, the glory of God to the surrounding nations of the world. The kingdom of David and Solomon provides a peek into a future heavenly kingdom, as the first part of the promise to Abraham is fulfilled. Israel, the world's first and only theocracy, embodies justice, righteousness, victory, peace, joy and happiness, prosperity, and wisdom, as well as safety from their enemies. Greater still is the building of a temple that is filled with the presence, even the glory, of the living God! And in this city of David, although the awe of God is there, the people gain assurance of salvation and forgiveness of their sins as they present to him their sacrifices of repentance and faith. And although, in time, God destroys this theocracy due to the constant failure and idolatries of many disobedient kings, he eventually restores the channel of redemption by bringing his captive people home to Zion, the city of God. Jerusalem is "the place" of sacrifice and its reestablishment paves the way for the coming of the messiah—the king—the Son of God, who is the only one worthy to die for the sins of his people. Jesus Christ is the fulfillment of the second part of the promise to Abraham. His incarnation, perfect life, profound words, death, resurrection, and ascension to the heavenly Father are the completion of act one in God's drama of redemption. Act two will follow, but that narrative will be left to the next volume.

Appendix One

"Ten Sure Ways to Leave
Your Pharaoh"

Brave Moses viewed the Pharaoh—greatest man on earth
God's staff was in his hand—he soon will learn its worth
His heart was very hardened—he'll regret his birth
There must be ten sure ways to leave your Pharaoh!

God's leader did not hesitate—he made the call . . .
(Furthermore) with Aaron by his side, he stood so strong and tall
"You let my people go"—God means every one and all
There must be ten sure ways to leave your Pharaoh!
. . . Ten sure ways to leave your Pharaoh!

Chorus:
Just turn the Nile red, Fred
Make all the frogs hop, Pop
Send a few gnats, Pat
And get yourself free . . .

Make all the flies swarm, Harm
Watch all the livestock drop!
Those boils on the skin, Ben
Sure would convince me!

Just let the flies swarm, Harm
Watch all the livestock drop
Those boils on the skin, Ben
Let God's people win!

(Just) drop down some hail, Gail
Let the locust invade, Wade
(And) bring on the dark, Mark
Let Israel embark!

When Pharaoh saw these signs—he wasn't too impressed;
(See this) his magic men with secret arts—they tried to do their best . . .
With one or two they shined—but baffled by the rest
They'll see the ten sure ways.

His heart was hard—God warned him well—he won't relent
No belief—there was no blood to save his son—he should repent
Finally let them go—but second guessing, his mighty troops he sent
There must be ten sure ways to leave your Pharaoh!
. . . Ten sure ways to leave your Pharaoh!

Repeat Chorus

Bibliography

Hatch, James "Buck." *Progress of Redemption* (Lecture Notes). CIU, 1979.

Keller, Tim. *Reason for God*. New York: Penguin, 2008.

Packer, J.I. *Knowing God*. Downers Grove: InterVarsity, 1973.

Scroggie, Graham. *The Unfolding Drama of Redemption*. Grand Rapids: Zondervan, 1970.

Made in the USA
Lexington, KY
17 April 2019